AI, Tell Me Your Protocol

Work Papers, Volume 9

Agustin V. Startari

Published by LEFORTUNE, 2026.

AI, TELL ME YOUR PROTOCOL

First edition. September 1, 2026.

ISBN: 979-8235352902

Written by Agustin V. Startari.

Table of Contents

In his work **"AI, Tell Me Your Protocols"** author **Agustin V. Startari** immerses us in a fascinating analysis of the intersection of technology and humanity in the era of big data. Exploring the rapid advancement of artificial intelligence (AI) and its impact on our society, the author invites us to reflect on the protocols that govern this relationship.

The book takes us on a journey through the world of big data and AI, unraveling key concepts and explaining how this technology has radically transformed the way we live, work, and interact. Startari examines the ethical, social, and economic implications of AI and raises fundamental questions about its integration into our daily lives.

From task automation to autonomous decision-making, the author examines how AI is permeating various fields such as industry, medicine, education, and commerce. Through concrete examples and case studies, the author shows how big data and algorithms are influencing our daily experience and how the protocols that guide their development and application can shape our future reality.

In his rigorous and analytical approach, Startari explores the concerns and ethical challenges that arise from the intersection of technology and humanity. He questions the power and responsibility of large technology companies and proposes limits and regulations to ensure that AI is used ethically and benefits society.

"AI, Tell Me Your Protocols" invites us to reflect on how we want AI to shape our world and how we can ensure a harmonious coexistence between technology and humanity. With an accessible style based on up-to-date research, Agustin V. Startari's book offers a profound and enlightening insight into the intersection of AI and humanity, challenging us to take an active role in shaping our technological future.

This collection gathers independent research works exploring power, ideology, legitimacy, and history through a cross-disciplinary lens. Each volume is self-contained yet contributes to a shared thread:

the critical analysis of how power is formed, exercised, and sustained over time. From Ancient Egypt to 20th-century totalitarianism, ***Work Papers*** presents a clear, academically grounded narrative about the historical and discursive mechanisms that shape our societies. Each entry is numbered to reflect its place in this evolving series.

Original Title: AI, Tell Me Your Protocol: The Intersection of Technology and Humanity in the Era of Big Data.

Series: WORK PAPERS #10

Cover Design: Visual Art Design

Editor: Jessica Yan, 2026

Publisher: LeFortune

ResearcherID: NGR-2476-2025

ORCID: 0009-0001-4714-6539

DOI: 10.5281/zenodo.15282728

http://dx.doi.org/10.2139/ssrn.5260083[1]

First Edition: May 2023

Second Edition: May 2025

Third Edition, Revised: 2026

LEFORTUNE

This publication should be cited as: Agustin V. Startari, "AI, Tell Me Your Protocol: The Intersection of Technology and Humanity in the Era of Big Data," WORKING PAPERS, 10, Montevideo, 2026 (rev. ed.).

1. https://dx.doi.org/10.2139/ssrn.5260083

Collection
WORK PAPERS
#10

PROLOGUE TO THE SECOND EDITION

Two years have passed since the publication of the first edition of *AI, Tell Me Your Protocol*, and in that short time, the field of artificial intelligence has evolved at a pace that continues to challenge the very frameworks through which we seek to understand its social, ethical, and economic consequences. The initial version of this work was conceived as a contribution to the ongoing dialogue about the intersection between technological innovation and human-centered values, with particular attention to the structural transformations in labor, governance, and cognition.

This second edition, completed in May 2025, emerges not only as an update but as a substantial revision. The urgency of the themes addressed in the original manuscript has only deepened with the global acceleration of AI deployment across domains. From the widespread experimentation with generative models and large language systems, to the institutional debates around the European Union AI Act and the proliferation of algorithmic management tools in workplaces, the social implications of artificial intelligence have become more tangible, more urgent, and more contested.

The updates to this edition are threefold. First, several chapters—particularly Chapter 2 on AI evaluation frameworks and Chapter 4 on sectoral transformations—have been significantly expanded to incorporate new empirical findings, updated bibliographic references from 2023 to 2025, and a more rigorous conceptual apparatus. Second, a new Chapter 5 has been introduced to examine the growing need for governance models that place human dignity, institutional accountability, and systemic foresight at the center of AI integration. Third, across the entire text, theoretical insights have been supplemented by data-driven analysis, comparative case studies, and policy-oriented reflection.

The audience for this work remains unchanged: researchers, policymakers, and practitioners interested in the transformative potential and complex risks of AI in the era of big data. As in the first edition, this is not a speculative account nor a technological manifesto. Rather, it is an effort to articulate the conditions under which AI may contribute to a more equitable and sustainable society—and the risks we face if we fail to engage critically with the systems we are rapidly deploying.

In preparing this second edition, I have sought to preserve the analytical clarity and academic integrity of the original, while responding to the evolving realities of a field marked by disruption, acceleration, and ethical ambiguity. The central question posed by this book remains as vital now as it was then: How can we ensure that artificial intelligence serves the human, rather than reshaping the human to serve the machine?

I thank the readers of the first edition for their constructive feedback and engagement. This second edition is also for them.

Agustín V. Startari

Nassau, Bahamas — May 2025

NOTE TO THE REVISED EDITION, 2026

The prologue that precedes this note was written in May 2025 and is reproduced here unaltered. It should be read as a document of its moment, and the reader is invited to compare its expectations against what followed. That comparison is the reason for this revision.

The second edition closed with a question: how might we ensure that artificial intelligence serves the human rather than reshaping the human to serve the machine? The question was well posed and I do not withdraw it. But it presupposed an answer to a prior question that the edition left unexamined—what kind of operation these systems actually perform—and it is that prior question which the present revision addresses. The result is not a change of subject. It is the recognition that the book had been assembling an argument it had not yet stated.

The argument is stated now, in a new section of the Introduction and in the section that opens Chapter 1. Briefly: a system trained on historical data can project only the regularities it has already recorded. This is a property of inductive inference, not a deficiency of engineering, and it does not diminish with scale. What follows is that artificial intelligence functions less as an agent of transformation than as an instrument of accelerated conservation, consolidating inherited categories, hierarchies, and relative costs faster than institutions can examine them. The central risk of the present transition is therefore not technological unemployment but the closure of institutional futures: the replacement of judgment, which can break a rule, by prediction, which can only extend one.

I arrived at this position by rereading my own conclusion. The claim was already there, in three passages I had written without recognizing that they formed a single thesis—one on the tendency of statistical models to inhibit creative rupture, one on the erosion of interpretative responsibility among those who defer to algorithmic output, and one on the relative cost of capital and labor as an institutional artifact rather than a technical fact. The chapters that follow have not been rewritten to accommodate this argument; they are its evidence, and they always were. What the revision supplies is the frame that makes them legible as such.

Three developments since May 2025 bear directly on the thesis, and I record them here because each could have refuted it.

The first is regulatory. The European Union's Artificial Intelligence Act, discussed in the second edition as a prospective instrument, has since entered into force in stages: its prohibitions in February 2025, its obligations for general-purpose models in August 2025, and its general application in August 2026. The obligations governing high-risk systems—conformity assessment, data governance, human oversight—were scheduled for that same date and were deferred, by the Digital Omnibus on AI, to December 2027 and August 2028. The pattern rewards attention. The duties that survived implementation were those requiring disclosure of how a system operates. The duties deferred were those requiring an institution to determine whether it should operate that way at all. Visibility held; revisability did not. I had not anticipated so exact a demonstration, and Chapter 5 has been revised accordingly.

The second is empirical, and it arrived from a direction I would not have chosen. The published findings of Brynjolfsson, Li, and Raymond on generative assistance in customer service report a substantial productivity gain concentrated among less experienced workers, with negligible gains—and a slight deterioration in output quality—among the most skilled. The result is generally read as evidence that these tools compress inequality by raising the floor. So they may. But the mechanism the authors identify is the dissemination of practices extracted from past performance, and its aggregate effect is convergence upon a historical mean. The floor rose because prior competence was distributed more widely; the ceiling fell slightly because the most capable were drawn toward a norm derived from a period in which they were exceptional. Whether this constitutes improvement depends on whether that mean deserved to be the target—a question no productivity metric is equipped to ask. I know of no better illustration of the thesis, and it was not produced to support it.

The third is the emergence of systems that reason across extended chains of inference before answering. If any development threatened the argument, this was the candidate, and I have considered it seriously. My conclusion is that it does not: extended inference searches more thoroughly within a space of learned regularities without acquiring the capacity to originate a category absent from that space. Depth of search is not novelty of category. I state the reasoning explicitly in Chapter 1 rather than in a footnote, because a thesis that cannot survive its strongest counter-example does not deserve to be defended, and the reader is entitled to judge whether it survives this one.

A word on what this revision does not do. It does not soften the second edition's conclusions, nor withdraw its recommendations, nor claim that the earlier text was mistaken. The survey it conducted was sound and the evidence it assembled remains the evidence. What has changed is that the book now argues rather than reports, and an argument incurs obligations a survey does not: it must state the conditions under which it would be wrong. Those conditions are specified in the Introduction. Should generative systems be shown to originate categories genuinely absent from their training distributions, the thesis fails, and I would rather it fail on stated terms than survive on unstated ones.

The question with which the second edition ended has not been answered here. It has been given a prior question on which its answer depends: whether the societies now deploying these systems will retain the institutional capacity to decide that some part of what they have inherited ought to be otherwise. On present evidence the question remains open, which is the only honest thing to say about it.

Agustin V. Startari
Nassau, Bahamas — 2026

INTRODUCTION

Artificial Intelligence (AI) has assumed a pivotal role in current academic, economic, and political discussions, given its potential to reshape the foundations of both productivity and social organization. Over the past decade, accelerated advances in AI have been made possible by the convergence of several key technological developments: the exponential growth of data availability—commonly referred to as big data—, the enhancement of computational processing power, and the refinement of algorithmic techniques, particularly in the domains of machine learning and deep learning. Moreover, the deployment of increasingly efficient and cost-accessible sensors has enabled AI systems to collect and process more precise and voluminous streams of environmental data. This has opened the door for AI integration into areas of activity that historically required human cognitive or sensory intervention. Tasks such as visual recognition, speech comprehension, and contextual decision-making—once considered exclusive to human intelligence—are now within the operational capabilities of advanced AI models.

A paradigmatic milestone in this trajectory is the 2016 victory of AlphaGo, an AI system developed by DeepMind, over world champion Lee Sedol in the strategic board game Go. Unlike prior forms of automation, which operated based on fixed inputs and predefined rules, current AI systems distinguish themselves by their ability to learn and improve autonomously through iterative exposure to data. This adaptive learning capacity not only enhances performance over time but also expands the potential domains in which AI can be applied (Jordan & Mitchell, 2015).

As a result, the horizon of technological feasibility has shifted. Applications once deemed implausible—such as fully autonomous vehicles—are now being prototyped and tested in real-world conditions, signaling the dawn of a new era in the automation of complex decision-making. While the timeline for general AI surpassing human intelligence across domains remains a subject of ongoing scholarly debate, it is technically plausible that, within the coming decades, AI will reach or exceed many of the benchmarks traditionally used to define human cognitive superiority. In this context, the need to analyze AI not only as a technical tool but also as a socio-political force becomes imperative. Its implications reach far beyond the domain of science and engineering, penetrating the fields of ethics, labor economics, surveillance, and governance. This book addresses that intersection. It is important to note that while all technology is inherently fallible and the pace of scientific progress remains uncertain, the potential of artificial intelligence (AI) to transform our collective reality is both impressive and unprecedented. This technological evolution challenges us not only to anticipate and adapt to future disruptions, but also to envision and design the conditions under which such a transformation can occur equitably and ethically.

AI constitutes a powerful and cross-cutting technology whose applications span an expanding array of domains, including—but not limited to—healthcare, finance, logistics, education, transportation, agriculture, and industrial production. One of the defining features of AI is its capacity for self-improvement through iterative learning, a trait that positions it as a so-called *general-purpose technology*—that is, a foundational innovation capable of catalyzing complementary advancements across multiple sectors (Brynjolfsson & McAfee, 2014). This versatility has generated significant attention from the academic, corporate, and governmental sectors alike, not merely because of its technical sophistication, but due to the profound systemic shifts it could provoke in labor dynamics, economic competitiveness, and institutional governance. Indeed, numerous economists and historians of technology have drawn parallels between the disruptive capacity of AI and previous transformative epochs in human history, such as those marked by the advent of electricity or the steam engine (Mokyr, 1990; Acemoglu & Restrepo, 2018).

Nevertheless, the projections surrounding AI are not devoid of controversy. On one end of the spectrum, optimists underscore the opportunities for innovation, economic growth, and improved human well-being. On the other, critics warn of existential risks, including the so-called *technological singularity*—a hypothetical scenario in which AI systems evolve beyond human control and comprehension (Bostrom, 2014). Although such projections remain speculative, there is widespread consensus that AI will significantly alter labor markets. The degree and direction of that impact, however, are far from settled.

The discourse surrounding the effects of AI on employment reveals a complex and multidimensional picture. While some studies anticipate the creation of new roles and industries, others highlight risks of job displacement, work intensification, task fragmentation, and the erosion of human-centered social relations in the workplace. Additionally, public opinion surveys in multiple countries have revealed increasing levels of anxiety regarding automation, surveillance, and the ethical dilemmas associated with algorithmic decision-making (Eurofound, 2018).

These concerns are not confined to the economic domain but extend to broader ethical and legal questions: Who is accountable when AI systems fail? How is personal data protected in algorithmic environments? To what extent do individuals retain agency in contexts mediated by opaque technological systems? Importantly, technological evolution is not deterministic. The trajectory of AI deployment will be shaped by a constellation of factors, including legal and regulatory frameworks, macroeconomic conditions, demographic shifts, educational adaptation, and—critically—the social acceptance of new technologies. In this regard, it becomes essential to frame the future not as a predetermined outcome but as a space of collective construction. Governments and institutions thus bear the responsibility to make informed, transparent, and inclusive decisions regarding AI's integration into the world of work. These decisions should foster a civic understanding of AI, enhance technological literacy, and ensure that its benefits are distributed equitably across society. Crucially, public authorities must establish robust safeguards in domains such as safety, liability, and algorithmic accountability, while fostering economic and social adaptability. The future of labor will not follow a single, linear path. Rather, it will emerge from the complex interaction of technological capacity, institutional response, and societal values. To this end, the responsible design of AI systems must be matched by equally thoughtful strategies of implementation and governance.

This book sets out to examine artificial intelligence not as an abstract or idealized phenomenon, but as a material and contingent technology—one whose capabilities are real but bounded, and whose impact will depend on the decisions and structures that accompany it. By clarifying what AI can—and cannot—do in the foreseeable future, we aim to support organizations, researchers, and policymakers in formulating strategies that balance innovation with human dignity, efficiency with inclusion, and progress with accountability. Secondly, this study will examine the measurable impacts of artificial intelligence on employment, wages, and occupational structures within the framework of current economic research. A critical review of the empirical evidence will be conducted to identify the main lessons drawn so far, while also proposing new lines of inquiry and methodological approaches to better capture the evolving nature of work in the age of AI. Sector-specific case studies will be introduced to illustrate the heterogeneity of these transformations, offering a more granular and multidimensional understanding of how AI reconfigures labor markets across different industries.

In the following chapters, we will also explore the ways in which AI is reshaping the content of work, altering how individuals collaborate with each other and with intelligent systems. Special attention will be given to the impact of AI on professional learning trajectories, the evolution of occupational identities, and the dynamic interplay between task substitution and task complementarity. These transformations raise fundamental questions about the nature of skill acquisition, the transmission of knowledge, and the future of human-machine interaction.

Finally, the book will present an integrated discussion of the major challenges that emerge from these developments, offering evidence-based recommendations for key stakeholders—including governments, international organizations, labor unions, the private sector, and civil society. It is imperative to develop a coordinated strategy that reflects the expectations and rights of citizens, establishes robust frameworks of accountability and cybersecurity, and guides technological change in a manner that promotes cohesion, equity, and long-term sustainability. In this sense, AI should not be passively received but actively shaped through inclusive and deliberative governance.

The Central Thesis: Artificial Intelligence Automates the Past

THE PRECEDING PAGES have surveyed a field. This section states an argument, and it is an argument that runs against the prevailing consensus.

The dominant framing of artificial intelligence—shared, remarkably, by its most enthusiastic advocates and its most alarmed critics—holds that AI is a disruptive force. The optimists welcome the disruption and the pessimists fear it, but both accept its premise: that these systems introduce something genuinely new into economic and institutional life, and that the task of governance is therefore to manage novelty. Nearly the entire policy apparatus assembled over the past decade rests on this shared assumption.

This book argues that the premise is mistaken, and that the error is consequential.

A system trained on historical data can only project regularities that have already occurred. This is not a defect of implementation to be corrected by better engineering or larger corpora; it is a constitutive property of statistical inference from past observation. Whatever such a system produces—a diagnosis, a credit decision, a hiring recommendation, a sentence of prose—is a reweighting of what has already been recorded. The apparent novelty of the output conceals the structural conservatism of the procedure that generated it.

From this follows the central claim of this volume: artificial intelligence does not automate work so much as it automates the past. Its deployment operates not as a force of transformation but as one of accelerated conservation. It consolidates existing occupational categories, entrenched hierarchies, prevailing relative costs, and inherited definitions of competent practice—and it does so at a velocity that outpaces the capacity of institutions to examine, contest, or revise them. The regularities of one period become the operating parameters of the next before anyone has determined whether they deserved to survive.

The consequence is that the central risk of the present transition has been misidentified. That risk is not technological unemployment, which is measurable, historically familiar, and susceptible to compensatory policy. It is the closure of institutional futures: the progressive substitution of judgment, which retains the capacity to break a rule, by prediction, which can only extend one. A society that has delegated its consequential decisions to systems structurally incapable of departing from precedent has not merely automated its labor. It has foreclosed its own revision.

Three properties of this thesis warrant emphasis at the outset. First, it is refutable, and the terms of its refutation are specifiable: were generative systems shown to produce genuine conceptual rupture rather than recombination—were they demonstrated to originate categories absent from their training distribution—the argument would fail. It is offered here as a proposition to be tested against evidence, not as a conviction to be asserted.

Second, it inverts the governance problem rather than restating it. If AI is disruptive, the appropriate institutional response is restraint: rules that slow deployment, contain harm, and buy time for adaptation. If AI is conservative in the sense argued here, restraint is precisely the wrong instrument, because the danger is not that things will change too fast but that they will cease to be capable of changing at all. What is required is not a brake but a mechanism of deliberate revision—institutional capacity to interrogate and overturn the inherited regularities that these systems are busy making permanent. The regulatory architecture assembled to date is calibrated for the wrong failure mode.

Third, the thesis reorganizes rather than discards the evidence assembled in the chapters that follow. Chapter 1 establishes the epistemological boundary from which the argument proceeds: what these systems can and cannot do, and why the limitation is structural rather than provisional. Chapter 2 demonstrates that prevailing evaluation frameworks measure fidelity to historical benchmarks and are therefore constitutionally unable to detect the conservation effect, being themselves instruments of it. Chapter 3 shows that the persistent failure of employment forecasting is not a defect of method but a symptom: projections fail because they extrapolate occupational categories that the technology is simultaneously freezing. Chapter 4 examines three sectors—healthcare, transportation, and banking—in which the pace and shape of adoption are determined not by technical capability but by institutionally constructed relative costs. Chapter 5 addresses what governance would require if the diagnosis offered here is correct. Chapter 6 draws the argument together and states its consequences.

The question this book pursues, then, is not whether artificial intelligence will transform work. It is whether the societies deploying it will retain the institutional capacity to decide that any part of the arrangement they have inherited ought to be otherwise.

CHAPTER 1: EXPLORING THE BOUNDARIES OF ARTIFICIAL INTELLIGENCE: POTENTIAL AND CHALLENGES

Artificial Intelligence (AI) emerged as a distinct scientific discipline in the mid-20th century, closely tied to the nascent field of computer science. Its foundational objective has been the design of computational systems capable of emulating human cognitive functions such as learning, reasoning, perception, and decision-making. The term artificial intelligence was first introduced in 1956 during the Dartmouth Summer Research Project, a seminal event organized by John McCarthy, Marvin Minsky, Nathaniel Rochester, and Claude Shannon. Among its early architects, figures such as McCarthy himself, Allen Newell, and Herbert A. Simon laid the groundwork for symbolic AI and heuristic problem-solving approaches (Russell & Norvig, 2010).

Since then, AI has undergone profound transformations, expanding to include diverse paradigms such as expert systems, probabilistic models, genetic algorithms, and—most notably in recent decades—machine learning and its subfield, deep learning. While the ambitions of early AI research often exceeded the technical limitations of the time, the convergence of three critical factors in the 21st century has significantly accelerated progress in the field: the exponential growth of available data (big data), the increased capacity of computing systems (especially through GPUs), and the development of multilayer artificial neural networks with high abstraction capabilities (Chollet, 2018; Goodfellow, Bengio, & Courville, 2016).

Machine learning, broadly defined, refers to a set of computational methods that enable systems to improve performance on a task through exposure to data, without being explicitly programmed for each case.

Within this framework, supervised learning has become the most prevalent model in industrial applications. This approach involves training neural networks on vast datasets of manually labeled input-output pairs, enabling the system to learn generalizable patterns and apply them to new, unseen data. Tasks such as image and speech recognition—once believed to be exclusive domains of human intelligence—can now be performed with remarkable accuracy by AI systems, largely due to advances in deep learning (LeCun, Bengio, & Hinton, 2015).

The implications of this evolution are profound. Just as the steam engine, electric motor, and programmable computers mechanized physical and symbolic labor in previous industrial revolutions, today's AI systems extend the frontier of automation into cognitive domains. Model-based classification processes now operate across diverse formats—visual, auditory, linguistic—ushering in a new era in which machines increasingly perform complex perceptual and inferential tasks. As Chollet (2018) notes, this shift is not merely quantitative but qualitative, altering the very nature of what machines are capable of doing.

Nevertheless, the capacity of AI systems to emulate certain aspects of human intelligence should not be mistaken for genuine understanding or consciousness. As Russell and Norvig (2010) emphasize, the appearance of intelligence in applications such as chatbots or recommendation engines should be carefully distinguished from autonomous reasoning or moral agency. Current AI models remain bounded by their architecture, training data, and design constraints.

Interest in AI has grown not only because of its technical potential, but also due to its wide-ranging applications across multiple sectors. In medicine, for example, AI supports diagnostic imaging and personalized treatment plans; in education, it facilitates adaptive learning platforms; in industry, it optimizes logistics and predictive maintenance (Brynjolfsson & McAfee, 2014). At the same time, the deployment of AI technologies raises critical ethical and regulatory questions, particularly in relation to privacy, algorithmic bias, and the concentration of technological power (Domingos, 2018).

A full understanding of AI therefore requires familiarity not only with its technical dimensions—such as machine learning and deep learning—but also with its geopolitical and socio-economic context. Nations such as China have become prominent actors in the AI race, mobilizing state-led strategies and investment policies to compete with long-established hubs like Silicon Valley (Lee, 2018). The global landscape of AI development thus reflects both collaboration and competition, innovation and regulation.

In conclusion, AI constitutes a dynamic and rapidly evolving field whose impact reaches far beyond the laboratory. Its promise to enhance efficiency and productivity must be weighed against its ethical, social, and institutional consequences. The present study adopts a realist approach to AI: one that neither overstates its capacities nor dismisses its transformative potential, but seeks instead to analyze how it is reshaping the boundaries of human labor, knowledge, and responsibility.

1.1 The Epistemological Boundary: Induction, Precedent, and the Structure of Machine Inference

BEFORE EXAMINING WHAT artificial intelligence accomplishes in application, it is necessary to establish with precision what kind of operation it performs. The distinction matters because a great deal of confusion in the policy literature follows from treating a limitation of principle as a limitation of degree—as an engineering deficit that additional data, parameters, or computation might eventually remedy.

The systems under discussion in this volume, whatever their architecture, share a single epistemological structure: they induce. They derive parameters from a corpus of prior observation and apply those parameters to cases not yet seen. Supervised learning generalizes from labeled precedent. Self-supervised language modeling estimates the conditional probability of a token given its context, where both the vocabulary and the distribution are inherited from a fixed body of recorded text. Reinforcement learning from human feedback substitutes one historical signal—expressed human preference—for another. In no case does the procedure contain a mechanism for originating a category that the training distribution does not already contain, however implicitly.

This is worth stating plainly, because the sophistication of contemporary output invites the opposite inference. A model that composes a competent legal brief, produces a diagnostic hypothesis, or generates an image in an unfamiliar style appears to be doing something more than reweighting precedent. It is not. Recombination across an extremely high-dimensional space is capable of generating outputs no human has encountered, and the subjective experience of novelty is genuine. But novelty of output is not the same as novelty of category. The space within which recombination occurs was fixed when the corpus was assembled.

The philosophical difficulty here is old, and naming it clarifies what is at stake. Hume observed that induction cannot justify itself: no quantity of past regularity entails its own continuation. Later formulations sharpened the problem—Goodman's demonstration that indefinitely many incompatible generalizations are consistent with any finite body of evidence, and the recognition in statistical learning theory that generalization is possible only under an assumption of distributional stability. Every operating machine learning system therefore embeds a substantive premise about the world: that the future will resemble the recorded past in the respects the model has learned to weight.

When that premise holds, the system performs well and its outputs are useful. When it fails, the system fails—and the failure has a characteristic signature. The literature terms it distributional shift and treats it as a robustness problem, a matter of graceful degradation under changing conditions. That framing is too narrow. The deeper point is normative rather than technical: whenever the world ought to change, a system trained on the world as it was will resist the change, and will do so with the full authority of statistical validation behind it. A model that has learned which candidates were historically hired, which neighborhoods were historically policed, which patients historically received treatment, or which prose historically counted as competent, encodes those arrangements as regularities. Asked to evaluate a departure from them, it registers the departure as improbable—which is to say, as error.

Here lies the asymmetry between machine inference and human judgment that organizes the argument of this book. Human judgment is also substantially inductive; experience shapes expectation, and precedent carries weight in human reasoning as it does in machine reasoning. But human judgment retains a faculty that inductive systems structurally lack: it can recognize a regularity as unjust and refuse it on that ground. The physician can depart from the guideline. The judge can distinguish the precedent. The examiner can conclude that the historical standard was wrong. This capacity for principled rule-breaking is not an incidental feature of human cognition to be optimized away as noise; it is the mechanism by which institutions revise themselves, and it has no counterpart in a procedure whose only access to normativity is the frequency with which something has previously occurred.

The empirical record now offers direct confirmation of the mechanism, and from an unexpected direction. Brynjolfsson, Li, and

Raymond (2025), studying the staggered deployment of a generative assistant across more than five thousand customer-service agents, report an average productivity gain of approximately fifteen percent, concentrated among novice and lower-skilled workers, who improved by roughly thirty percent, while gains among experienced high-skill workers were small—accompanied by a small decline in the quality of their output. The authors attribute the pattern to the model's dissemination of the tacit practices of more capable workers.

The finding is typically read as encouraging: a technology that compresses inequality by raising the floor. Read against the argument advanced here, it describes something more equivocal. The system did not generate new practice; it propagated existing practice, extracted from historical performance. The floor rose because past competence was distributed more widely. The ceiling fell, slightly, because the most capable practitioners were drawn toward a norm derived from a period in which they were the exception. The aggregate effect is convergence on the historical mean—precisely what an inductive system distributed across an organization should be expected to produce. Whether such convergence constitutes improvement depends entirely on whether the historical mean deserved to be the target, and that is a question the system cannot pose and the productivity metric cannot register.

Three objections merit direct response.

The first holds that scale dissolves the limitation: a sufficiently large model trained on a sufficiently broad corpus approximates the space of all expressible thought, rendering the distinction between recombination and origination academic. But scale enlarges the space of recombination without altering its character, and it aggravates the concern rather than relieving it. A larger corpus is a larger deposit of the past. It encodes more regularities, weighted more confidently, and therefore exerts a stronger conservative pull. Scale increases the authority of precedent; it does not introduce a faculty for departing from it.

I have examined this question at length elsewhere, from the standpoint of attribution rather than epistemology (Startari 2026a). What that analysis establishes is that generative systems produce what may be termed synthetic originality: outputs that satisfy every operational test of novelty while consisting entirely of probabilistic recombination of absorbed human production. The mechanism is worth stating precisely, because it explains why the scale objection feels compelling and is nonetheless mistaken. Attribution does not collapse because sources are absent from the training corpus; it collapses because the output dissolves the reconstructible link between intellectual origin and textual manifestation. The novelty is real at the level of the artifact and absent at the level of the category. Scale intensifies this: a larger corpus yields outputs less traceable to any particular precedent while remaining, in aggregate, more thoroughly determined by precedent as such. What increases with scale is not the capacity to originate but the difficulty of demonstrating that origination has not occurred.

The second objection points to reinforcement learning, to systems that discover strategies no human devised—the archetypal case being the game-playing programs whose innovations reshaped expert practice in Go and chess. This objection has genuine force, and the concession should be explicit: within a formally closed domain, where the rules are complete and the objective is exactly specifiable, machine search can and does originate strategy beyond human precedent. But the condition is doing the work. Such systems innovate within a rule set they cannot question, toward an objective they did not select. They are superlative at discovering unnoticed consequences of fixed rules and structurally incapable of asking whether the rules should be fixed as they are. Labor markets, clinical practice, credit allocation, and public administration are not closed domains. In these settings the rules themselves are the contested object, the objective function is precisely what is under negotiation, and the relevant form of innovation is the one that revises the rules rather than exploiting them.

The argument advanced here converges with a conclusion I have reached elsewhere by a different route, and the convergence is worth recording because the two lines of inquiry are independent. In Colonization of Time (Startari 2025c) and Executable Power (Startari 2025b), I approached predictive infrastructures through the analysis of syntax rather than epistemology, asking how the form of machine-generated language acquires binding force. That analysis concludes that predictive systems do not forecast futures but substitute them: once a model's conditions are satisfied, its output does not advise a decision but executes one, so that optimization displaces exploration and the task ceases to be the imagination of alternatives and becomes the minimization of error relative to past data. The vocabulary there is structural, concerned with what I termed the compiled rule and the executable sovereign. The vocabulary here is epistemological, concerned with induction and precedent. The conclusion is the same, and it is reached without the one argument depending on the other: a system whose only access to the future runs through the recorded past narrows what can be attempted, and it does so by operation rather than by intent. Two distinct routes arriving at one destination is weak evidence for a thesis, but it is not no evidence, and I note it as such.

The third objection is the most recent and, in my judgment, the most serious. Since 2024 a class of systems has appeared that does not emit an answer directly but generates an extended intermediate chain of inference before responding, allocating additional computation at the moment of use rather than only during training. On several classes of problem—mathematical, logical, and programmatic—these systems substantially outperform their predecessors, and they do so in a manner that resembles deliberation closely enough to warrant the question: if a system can reason through a problem step by step, revising its own intermediate conclusions, has it not acquired something like the capacity for judgment that the preceding argument reserves to human beings?

The question deserves a better answer than a restatement of the thesis. Let me grant what should be granted. Extended inference is not a cosmetic advance. It permits the composition of longer derivational chains, the detection of certain of the system's own errors, and the exploration of a considerably larger portion of the space of possible solutions than single-pass generation allows. Where a problem has a determinate answer reachable by a sequence of valid steps, these systems find answers their predecessors did not.

But consider what the additional computation is spent on. It searches. It searches a space of learned regularities more thoroughly, more persistently, and with better error-correction than before, and the space it searches is the one that training established. Depth of search is not novelty of category. A system that explores a region exhaustively has not thereby acquired the capacity to recognize that the region is the wrong one, and the self-correction such systems perform is correction against learned criteria of validity—it detects steps that are improbable given its training, not premises that are unjust given a norm it has never encountered. This is the same faculty examined above, applied with greater persistence.

The distinction can be put in terms of the earlier discussion of closed domains. Extended inference is most impressive precisely where the domain is closed: mathematics, formal logic, code that either compiles or does not. In those settings the criteria of correctness are complete and internal, and a system that searches deeply against complete criteria will find what shallower search missed. The problems this book concerns itself with—whether an occupational category should persist, whether a historical hiring pattern should govern future hiring, whether a relative cost reflects anything but institutional arrangement—are not of that kind. Their criteria of correctness are external to any specification, contested among the parties they affect, and the object of the very deliberation at issue. A longer chain of inference from the same premises reaches further conclusions from those premises. It does not reach the question of whether the premises deserved to be adopted.

There is, moreover, a consideration that cuts against the objection rather than for it. A system that produces an extended and legible chain of reasoning is considerably more persuasive than one that produces a bare determination, and persuasiveness is not accuracy. The appearance of shown work invites the reader to audit the steps rather than to interrogate the starting point, and a chain of individually valid inferences from an unexamined premise is precisely the structure most likely to escape scrutiny. If the thesis of this book is correct, the arrival of systems that both conserve the past and appear to deliberate is not a mitigation of the problem it identifies. It is an intensification of it.

It is necessary at this point to distinguish the present argument from a body of criticism it superficially resembles, because the resemblance is close enough that a reader might reasonably take this book to be restating a position already established.

Several critics have argued that artificial intelligence functions to preserve rather than disturb existing arrangements. Katz (2020) contends that AI has served as an instrument of established power throughout its institutional history, its apparent novelty concealing continuity in whose interests it advances, and that the field's self-presentation as a neutral technical enterprise is itself part of the mechanism. Research collectives working on algorithmic accountability have argued that absent deliberate intervention, AI development will reproduce and entrench prevailing social hierarchies. In a related register, critics of predictive infrastructure have observed that when regulators, insurers, and firms rely on structurally similar models, the result is a form of model-driven conservatism that transfers risk onto those least able to absorb it, alongside a systemic fragility arising from correlated error.

These arguments are correct, and the present study does not dispute them. But they are arguments of a different kind, and the difference determines what follows from each.

The critiques just described locate the conservative tendency in the political economy of AI: in who funds it, who builds it, whose interests its objectives encode, and what ideological work its claim to neutrality performs. On this account the conservation is a consequence of interest and could in principle be otherwise. Different funders, different objectives, participatory design, a redistributed field, and the technology would conserve less, or conserve something else. The remedy implied is political, and it is the right remedy for the problem identified.

The argument of this book locates the conservative tendency one level further down, in the structure of inductive inference itself. On this account a system trained on recorded observation would exhibit the tendency even if its funders were disinterested, its objectives were benevolent, and its design were fully participatory—because the constraint is not whose past is encoded but that a past is encoded, and that projection from precedent cannot originate what precedent does not contain. The two accounts are compatible and mutually reinforcing: the political critique explains whose arrangements are conserved, and the epistemological argument explains why conservation occurs at all. Neither substitutes for the other.

Evidence for the operational reading, as distinct from the intentional one, is available from a direction that might not be expected. In work analyzing how generative systems handle geopolitical material (Startari 2026b), I have argued that inherited hierarchies can be reproduced through entirely ordinary textual operations—compression, recontextualization, nominalization, agent deletion, lexical selection, source weighting—without any explicit ideological commitment on the part of the system or its designers. The finding matters here because it separates the two accounts empirically rather than merely conceptually. If conservation required interest, it would appear where interest is present and be absent where interest is not. If it follows from the structure of the operations themselves, it will appear in the ordinary functioning of systems whose designers hold no relevant position at all, which is what the analysis of those cases indicates.

The consequence of taking the epistemological route is that the remedy changes. If conservation follows from interest, correcting the interest is sufficient. If it follows from the structure of inference, no correction of interest will remove it, and the requirement becomes institutional rather than technical: a capacity to periodically reconsider and overturn what the systems have encoded, maintained deliberately, because nothing in the technology will supply it. This is why the governance argument developed in Chapter 6 diverges from the recommendations that ordinarily accompany the political critique. It is also why the thesis is falsifiable in a way that critiques of interest are not, since it stands or falls on a claim about what inductive systems can do rather than on a claim about whom they serve.

This, then, is the epistemological boundary from which the remainder of this book proceeds. It is not a claim that these systems are ineffective, nor that their outputs lack value, nor that human cognition is mystically exempt from computational description. It is a narrower and more consequential claim: that inductive systems can only conserve, that they conserve at a speed and scale no prior technology of precedent has approached, and that the institutional consequences of this property have been almost entirely overlooked by a literature preoccupied with disruption. The sections that follow examine the domains in which this property is now operating.

1.2 Applied Artificial Intelligence: Domains, Achievements, and Limitations

THE PRACTICAL APPLICATIONS of artificial intelligence (AI) have expanded rapidly in recent years, demonstrating measurable impacts across diverse domains such as healthcare, education, and finance. These sectors have become emblematic of how AI can enhance precision, personalization, and decision-making efficiency—while simultaneously exposing the ethical, infrastructural, and epistemological limitations of current technologies.

In the healthcare field, AI has shown remarkable utility in early disease detection and diagnostic support. A landmark study by Esteva et al. (2017) demonstrated that convolutional neural networks could match dermatologists in classifying skin cancer using photographic images of lesions. Similarly, Rajpurkar et al. (2017) developed the CheXNet model, a 121-layer convolutional neural network capable of detecting pneumonia from chest X-rays with radiologist-level accuracy. More recently, advancements have continued with transformer-based architectures such as BioGPT and Med-PaLM, developed by Microsoft and Google, respectively, to interpret clinical notes, triage decisions, and radiological data (Singhal et al., 2023).

In the education sector, AI is being applied to facilitate personalized learning experiences. Intelligent tutoring systems such as *Smart Sparrow* (VanLehn et al., 2005) and *ALEKS* (Assessment and Learning in Knowledge Spaces) use adaptive learning algorithms to tailor instructional content to students' progress, strengths, and preferences. More recently, large language models (LLMs) like GPT-4 have begun to serve as writing tutors, language partners, and even curriculum design assistants, although concerns remain regarding reliability and factual grounding (Zawacki-Richter et al., 2019).

In finance, AI is widely used in fraud detection, risk modeling, and portfolio optimization. Chen et al. (2016) developed a deep learning model to detect credit card fraud with high precision, using behavioral pattern recognition from large transaction datasets. Meanwhile, Crosby et al. (2017) demonstrated how neural networks can be trained to predict stock price trends and optimize investment strategies. These models have since evolved, with current AI trading systems incorporating reinforcement learning for real-time market adaptation (Zhang et al., 2021).

These applications reveal the significant contributions of AI to increased accuracy, efficiency, and personalization. However, they also highlight persistent limitations that must be addressed. One critical constraint is the computational intensity of AI systems. Training state-of-the-art deep learning models may require investments upwards of hundreds of thousands of dollars in cloud GPU computing, along with extensive energy consumption and carbon footprint (Jia, 2019; Patterson et al., 2021).

Another limitation lies in explainability. While AI systems can perform highly complex classification and prediction tasks, they often function as "black boxes," offering little to no transparency into how decisions are made. For instance, an image recognition model trained to distinguish between cats and dogs may perform well statistically, yet be entirely unable to provide a human-interpretable explanation of its classification logic (Russell & Norvig, 2010). This issue becomes particularly concerning in high-stakes domains such as medical diagnostics or financial fraud detection, where accountability and interpretability are essential (Doshi-Velez & Kim, 2017). In addition, AI systems are fundamentally constrained by the quality and representativeness of the data they are trained on. Biases embedded in training datasets can perpetuate or exacerbate inequalities, particularly in applications involving human profiling or predictive policing. The assumption that patterns learned from historical data will generalize to real-world contexts is often unwarranted, especially in dynamic or culturally sensitive environments (Barocas, Hardt, & Narayanan, 2019). Thus, while AI continues to make meaningful advances, it remains far from replicating the full scope of human reasoning, contextual understanding, and ethical deliberation. Its progress should be situated within a framework of critical realism—recognizing both the achievements and limitations of current systems, and pursuing a research agenda that emphasizes interpretability, robustness, and social accountability.

1.3 Current Limitations and the Irreplaceability of Human Intelligence

DESPITE THE IMPRESSIVE progress made in the field of artificial intelligence, several critical limitations continue to hinder its ability to replicate or surpass human intelligence in both complex and deceptively simple tasks. These constraints are primarily associated with the availability, quality, and representativeness of macrodata, as well as the epistemological opacity of AI systems that are not grounded in deterministic frameworks (Bostrom, 2017; LeCun, Bengio, & Hinton, 2015). Training advanced AI models—particularly deep learning architectures—requires immense computational resources and massive, meticulously curated datasets. The data must not only be annotated with human expertise but must also adequately represent the diversity and complexity of the real-world phenomena being modeled. Otherwise, the algorithm's outputs become unreliable or skewed. Furthermore, even well-trained systems often struggle to generalize beyond the distribution of their training data, leading to what is known as distributional shift, which compromises their robustness in novel contexts (Recht et al., 2019). One of the most pressing concerns in this context is the reproduction of algorithmic bias. When training data includes historical inequalities or structural discrimination, AI systems can perpetuate and even amplify those injustices. A well-known study by Obermeyer et al. (2019) revealed that a widely used healthcare algorithm exhibited significant racial bias by systematically underestimating the health needs of Black patients compared to white patients with similar clinical conditions. These biases raise serious questions about the legitimacy and fairness of algorithmic decision-making, particularly in sensitive domains such as healthcare, employment, credit scoring, and law enforcement (Barocas et al., 2019).

The technical and ethical challenges associated with these biases underscore the indispensable role of human oversight. Ensuring data quality and fairness requires considerable human intervention—not only during data collection and labeling but also during post-training validation and contextual interpretation. As Floridi et al. (2018) emphasize, trustworthy AI demands transparency, accountability, and continuous field testing to mitigate unintentional harms and ensure that system outputs align with normative human values. Moreover, the ambition of achieving general or "strong" AI—systems capable of understanding, learning, and reasoning across a wide variety of tasks and domains—remains far from realization. Today's AI operates almost exclusively within narrow or task-specific contexts. It excels at classification, prediction, or pattern recognition within defined parameters but lacks the cognitive flexibility, moral reasoning, and emotional depth that characterize human intelligence. As Gomila (2021) notes, AI systems function within deterministic environments and lack the capacity for true empathy or holistic social understanding. Their "intelligence" is context-bound and non-reflective, unable to adapt to the open-ended, nuanced, and dynamic nature of human relationships. This distinction is particularly important in domains that demand ethical deliberation, interpretive judgment, and empathy—capacities that remain, at present, exclusively human. While AI may support or augment decision-making, it cannot replace the inherently human dimensions of care, justice, and meaning-making. Brynjolfsson and McAfee (2014) rightly argue that AI can optimize well-defined tasks but lacks the meta-awareness and contextual reflexivity necessary for full autonomy. In this light, rather than pursuing the illusion of total automation, the more constructive path lies in designing hybrid systems in which AI complements human expertise. These systems should be built upon shared responsibility frameworks that preserve human agency while leveraging the computational advantages of machine intelligence.

CHAPTER 2: PERSPECTIVES ON THE EVALUATION OF AI IMPACT

Artificial intelligence (AI) constitutes an inherently interdisciplinary field at the intersection of computer science, cognitive science, mathematics, and engineering. Its principal objective is to develop systems capable of emulating or reproducing functions traditionally associated with human intelligence, such as perception, reasoning, decision-making, and learning. This endeavor involves not only the design of complex algorithms and data structures, but also the incorporation of models that can function in uncertain, dynamic, and socially embedded contexts.

The diverse approaches to AI can be broadly categorized into symbolic and sub-symbolic paradigms, each with its own historical lineage, epistemological assumptions, and domains of application.

2.1 Symbolic and Sub-symbolic Approaches to AI

SYMBOLIC ARTIFICIAL intelligence, commonly referred to as Good Old-Fashioned Artificial Intelligence (GOFAI), is founded on the principle that intelligent behavior can be modeled through the manipulation of abstract symbols governed by formal logical rules. This paradigm emerged from the physical symbol system hypothesis formulated by Newell and Simon in the 1970s, which posits that any system capable of intelligent action must operate on symbolic structures through rule-based transformations. Within this framework, knowledge is represented explicitly, allowing systems to perform reasoning through structured inference mechanisms. Techniques such as propositional logic, predicate logic, semantic networks, frames, and production rules constitute the core tools of symbolic AI.

Among the most influential implementations of symbolic AI were expert systems, which reached their peak in development and deployment during the 1980s and early 1990s. These systems encoded domain-specific expertise using a set of declarative "if-then" rules, processed through an inference engine capable of forward or backward chaining. Notable examples include MYCIN, a medical diagnosis system designed to identify bacterial infections and recommend treatments, and XCON, a rule-based configurator developed by Digital Equipment Corporation to automate the assembly of computer systems. These systems demonstrated that it was possible to formalize professional knowledge and automate decision-making in constrained domains (Russell & Norvig, 2010).

Despite their successes, symbolic AI systems encountered several limitations, particularly in dealing with incomplete, uncertain, or ambiguous information, and in scaling to real-world complexity. Their brittleness and reliance on manually crafted rule sets also made them costly to maintain and difficult to generalize beyond narrowly defined contexts. These constraints contributed to the eventual decline of GOFAI as the dominant paradigm, especially with the rise of statistical and data-driven approaches in the late 1990s and early 2000s. Nonetheless, recent advances in hybrid neuro-symbolic systems have revitalized interest in integrating symbolic reasoning with machine learning techniques, seeking to combine the transparency and formal rigor of symbolic methods with the flexibility and scalability of modern neural models (Besold et al., 2017; Marcus, 2020).

While symbolic artificial intelligence demonstrates strong performance in well-structured domains characterized by explicitly defined logic and constraints—such as legal reasoning, formal verification, or deterministic planning—its applicability diminishes when faced with environments involving ambiguity, uncertainty, or sensory complexity. These limitations prompted the development of alternative approaches better suited to dynamic and less formally defined problems. Sub-symbolic artificial intelligence, emerging from this need, diverges from explicit rule-based reasoning by leveraging statistical inference and adaptive learning from data.

Sub-symbolic AI encompasses a wide array of models that infer patterns without relying on predefined symbolic structures. These models include artificial neural networks, genetic algorithms, support vector machines, and hidden Markov models. Unlike symbolic systems, which require manual encoding of knowledge, sub-symbolic methods are designed to generalize from data, learning implicit representations through training. One of the most transformative advances in this domain is deep learning, which utilizes multilayered neural networks to capture complex, high-dimensional features in data sets. Convolutional neural networks (CNNs) have achieved state-of-the-art performance in visual recognition tasks, while recurrent neural networks (RNNs) and their successors—such as long short-term memory (LSTM) networks and transformers—have been pivotal in processing sequential data for applications including speech recognition, machine translation, and time-series forecasting (Goodfellow, Bengio, & Courville, 2016; Vaswani et al., 2017).

These sub-symbolic techniques have surpassed symbolic AI in many real-world applications, particularly in domains where patterns are latent, high-dimensional, or context-dependent. Natural language processing, computer vision, and autonomous systems are prominent examples in which statistical learning outperforms rule-based approaches. However, the widespread adoption of these models has introduced critical challenges related to interpretability. Deep learning models, in particular, are often regarded as "black boxes," as their internal representations and decision-making processes are not readily transparent or explainable. This opacity raises significant ethical and practical concerns, especially in high-stakes contexts such as medical diagnostics, criminal justice, or financial decision-making, where accountability, bias mitigation, and reliability are essential (Doshi-Velez & Kim, 2017; Lipton, 2018).

As the field advances, the tension between predictive accuracy and interpretability has become a central concern in AI research. Addressing this challenge requires novel frameworks that can balance the adaptability and scalability of sub-symbolic systems with the need for transparency, auditability, and alignment with human values.

2.2 Beyond Algorithms: Expanding the Scope of AI Evaluation

ARTIFICIAL INTELLIGENCE (AI) extends far beyond algorithmic design and computational models. Its contemporary scope encompasses a wide array of domains, including probabilistic reasoning, automated planning, computer vision, robotics, multi-agent systems, and human–computer interaction. These application areas are not merely technical in nature; they require the capacity to function within open, dynamic, and often unpredictable environments. As such, the success of AI systems in these domains is contingent not only upon computational performance but also on their capacity to adapt, interact, and operate safely and ethically in the real world.

With the growing deployment of AI systems in socially consequential contexts, the limitations of traditional evaluation metrics—such as precision, recall, F1-score, and computational efficiency—have become increasingly apparent. In areas such as healthcare diagnostics, judicial decision-making, algorithmic recruitment, financial risk assessment, and autonomous driving, performance cannot be divorced from broader societal consequences. Decisions made by AI systems in these domains have direct implications for human lives, civil liberties, and systemic equity (Eubanks, 2018; Mittelstadt et al., 2016). The need for holistic evaluation frameworks has therefore become a central concern in contemporary AI research and governance. These frameworks must integrate ethical, legal, and social dimensions into the development and assessment processes. Concepts such as fairness, accountability, transparency, and explainability—often abbreviated as FATE—have emerged as key principles for evaluating AI systems beyond their predictive power (Floridi et al., 2018; Selbst et al., 2019). For instance, a hiring algorithm that optimizes for accuracy but systematically disadvantages marginalized groups due to biased training data cannot be deemed acceptable, regardless of its technical performance. Moreover, the operational context of AI systems must be considered a critical part of their evaluation. An autonomous vehicle that performs well in controlled environments may fail under real-world conditions that involve unpredictable pedestrian behavior, weather variation, or ambiguous signage. Similarly, a diagnostic tool may show high accuracy in test environments but encounter severe limitations when deployed in low-resource healthcare systems due to infrastructure, user training, or cultural mismatches.

To address these challenges, researchers and policymakers are increasingly calling for interdisciplinary approaches that combine insights from computer science, law, ethics, and the social sciences. This involves not only designing technical safeguards but also engaging with affected communities, stakeholders, and domain experts throughout the lifecycle of AI systems. Participatory design, impact assessments, algorithmic audits, and ethical review boards are examples of tools that can help bridge the gap between algorithmic performance and social responsibility (Whittlestone et al., 2019; Jobin, Ienca, & Vayena, 2019). In sum, evaluating AI systems demands a shift from narrow, performance-centric metrics to comprehensive, context-aware frameworks that account for the broader consequences of intelligent automation. Such an expansion is essential for ensuring that AI systems serve not only efficiency and innovation but also justice, dignity, and democratic oversight.

2.3 The Central Challenges: Interpretability, Ethics, and Bias

INTERPRETABILITY REMAINS one of the most urgent and unresolved challenges in contemporary artificial intelligence (AI), particularly in relation to deep learning models. As AI systems increasingly adopt complex architectures—such as convolutional neural networks, transformers, and generative adversarial networks—their internal decision-making processes become opaque to both developers and end-users. This phenomenon, often referred to as the "black box" problem, undermines the ability to trace, explain, or justify model outputs, especially in high-stakes applications such as medical diagnostics, criminal sentencing, or credit approval (Doshi-Velez & Kim, 2017). In such contexts, lack of explainability is not a technical inconvenience but a normative deficit that compromises transparency, trust, and legal accountability. This lack of interpretability poses significant risks for democratic governance and rule-of-law principles. When individuals or institutions are subject to decisions made by algorithms they cannot interrogate or contest, foundational rights such as due process and equal protection under the law may be compromised. As a result, the demand for explainable AI (XAI) has surged across regulatory, technical, and ethical domains, pushing researchers to explore methods such as model distillation, local approximations (e.g., LIME or SHAP), and inherently interpretable model design (Rudin, 2019). In parallel, the ethics of AI has become a focal point of global academic and policy discourse. Among the central ethical concerns are algorithmic fairness, discrimination, privacy, surveillance, and the moral delegation of autonomous decisions. As machine learning systems are trained on large-scale datasets—often harvested from the web or institutional repositories—they risk inheriting and amplifying the historical and structural biases embedded within those datasets (Barocas, Hardt, & Narayanan, 2019). For example, predictive policing tools have been shown to disproportionately target marginalized communities, while hiring algorithms have inadvertently penalized women or ethnic minorities based on skewed training data (Angwin et al., 2016).

These risks are not merely technical flaws but reflect deeper socio-political asymmetries. Addressing them requires moving beyond mere algorithmic adjustments to interrogate the broader systems of data collection, representation, and institutional use. Moreover, privacy concerns have intensified as AI systems increasingly rely on surveillance infrastructures, biometric identification, and behavioral tracking. This has triggered renewed debates on data ownership, informed consent, and the limits of algorithmic profiling, particularly under legal regimes such as the General Data Protection Regulation (GDPR) and emerging AI legislation in the European Union (Veale & Edwards, 2018). Ethical AI also raises the question of moral agency: to what extent can or should autonomous systems make decisions in morally ambiguous situations? Autonomous vehicles, for instance, may face trolley problem-type scenarios requiring the weighing of lives under uncertainty. Such dilemmas underscore the necessity of embedding ethical reasoning into the design, deployment, and governance of AI technologies (Boddington, 2017).

Ultimately, ensuring that AI systems are interpretable, ethical, and bias-aware requires a convergence of technical rigor and normative reflection. It calls for interdisciplinary collaboration among computer scientists, legal scholars, ethicists, sociologists, and affected communities. It also demands institutional structures capable of oversight, redress, and public deliberation. Without such measures, the social legitimacy and long-term sustainability of AI innovations remain at risk.

2.4 Toward a Responsible AI

ARTIFICIAL INTELLIGENCE is not merely a technological discipline but a transformative socio-technical system whose influence extends across nearly every domain of public and private life. As AI systems increasingly shape decision-making processes in healthcare, finance, education, transportation, and governance, the development of responsible AI becomes a critical imperative. Responsibility in this context involves more than functional correctness or technical performance; it encompasses questions of accountability, transparency, equity, and societal alignment.

The integration of symbolic and sub-symbolic methods has allowed AI to address a growing array of real-world problems, from high-frequency trading to autonomous navigation and natural language understanding. However, the social consequences of these applications are often diffuse, cumulative, and difficult to predict. This underscores the need for an interdisciplinary framework for AI development—one that is informed not only by advances in computer science but also by insights from ethics, law, sociology, and political theory (Crawford & Calo, 2016).

A responsible approach to AI must therefore move beyond narrowly technical assessments and address the normative dimensions of system design and deployment. This includes establishing mechanisms for democratic oversight, ensuring procedural fairness in algorithmic processes, and protecting fundamental rights such as privacy, non-discrimination, and freedom of expression. Moreover, the principle of *proportionality* should guide the implementation of AI in contexts where its impact on individuals and institutions may be profound. Technologies that affect civil liberties, such as facial recognition or predictive analytics in criminal justice, require stricter standards of justification and public accountability (Whittaker et al., 2018).

Operationalizing responsible AI entails both ex ante and ex post governance. On the one hand, ex ante measures include ethical impact assessments, participatory design processes, and the adoption of transparency-enhancing tools such as model documentation (e.g., datasheets for datasets and model cards). On the other hand, ex post governance involves mechanisms for auditability, algorithmic redress, and institutional liability for AI-related harms (Brundage et al., 2020). Furthermore, responsible AI must be globally informed yet locally grounded. While international organizations such as the OECD,

UNESCO, and the European Commission have proposed normative frameworks for ethical AI, the concrete implementation of these principles must be sensitive to contextual differences in law, culture, and institutional capacity. In regions with weaker regulatory institutions, the risk of technological colonization—where AI systems developed elsewhere are deployed without sufficient adaptation—remains high.

Ultimately, evaluating what AI *can* do must be complemented by a careful deliberation about what AI *ought* to do. This requires a shift in research and policy priorities: from optimization and scalability to reflection and restraint; from efficiency to legitimacy; from control to cooperation. Without such a paradigm, the full promise of artificial intelligence may be overshadowed by unintended consequences and social fragmentation.

CHAPTER 3: AI AND EMPLOYMENT — BETWEEN JOB DISPLACEMENT AND TRANSFORMATION

The adoption of artificial intelligence (AI) in the workplace presents a complex interplay of opportunities and risks for workers, enterprises, and public institutions. On one hand, the automation of repetitive, dangerous, or cognitively taxing tasks offers the promise of increased productivity, reduced occupational hazards, and the reallocation of human effort toward higher-value activities. In this sense, AI can contribute to improving job quality by freeing workers from monotonous routines and enhancing workplace safety in sectors such as manufacturing, logistics, and healthcare (Autor, 2015; Bessen, 2019).

On the other hand, these technological advances are not without significant structural challenges. The introduction of AI systems often leads to the displacement of workers in occupations where tasks can be fully or partially automated, particularly in clerical, administrative, and routine-intensive roles. As machines become capable of performing cognitive functions once thought to be exclusive to humans—such as language processing, decision-making under uncertainty, and visual recognition—the range of at-risk jobs continues to expand (Frey & Osborne, 2017; Brynjolfsson & Mitchell, 2017).

Moreover, the reconfiguration of tasks within occupations introduces the problem of skill obsolescence. Workers may find their competencies misaligned with the demands of AI-augmented workplaces, where digital literacy, data analysis, and cross-functional collaboration become increasingly central. The resulting skill mismatch can exacerbate existing labor market inequalities, particularly affecting low-skilled workers and those in precarious employment (Chui et al., 2018).

Organizational redesign is another major consequence of AI integration. Firms adopting AI must adapt their workflows, decision-making processes, and human resource strategies to accommodate the new technological environment. This includes redefining job roles, reallocating responsibilities between humans and machines, and investing in reskilling and change management programs. The capacity of firms to implement these changes equitably and effectively will largely determine the social and economic outcomes of AI adoption.

Therefore, the integration of AI into the workplace must be accompanied by proactive governance, including robust labor policies, continuous training systems, and inclusive innovation strategies. Without coordinated efforts between employers, governments, and civil society, the benefits of AI may be concentrated among a few actors, while the social costs are broadly distributed. A human-centered approach to technological transition, grounded in social dialogue and institutional support, is essential to ensure that AI serves as a complement to human labor rather than its replacement.

3.1 Opportunities: Task Enhancement and Workplace Safety

THE INTEGRATION OF artificial intelligence (AI) into the workplace introduces a range of transformative opportunities that extend beyond mere automation. One of the most immediate and tangible benefits lies in the capacity of AI systems to perform repetitive, physically demanding, or hazardous tasks, thereby improving both efficiency and occupational safety. In industrial settings, for instance, AI-powered robots are increasingly employed in environments that pose risks to human health—such as high-temperature manufacturing, chemical handling, or heavy lifting—thereby reducing workplace injuries and enabling compliance with stringent safety regulations (De Stefano & Wouters, 2020; International Labour Organization, 2023).

Beyond physical safety, the reallocation of routine or low-complexity tasks to machines allows human workers to engage in more cognitively demanding and emotionally complex activities. These include strategic decision-making, creative problem-solving, and interpersonal communication, which are difficult to automate and contribute significantly to job satisfaction and individual well-being. Empirical studies have shown that the enrichment of task content—when supported by adequate training and organizational support—can lead to higher productivity, stronger employee engagement, and improved service quality, particularly in sectors such as healthcare, education, and professional services (Arntz, Gregory, & Zierahn, 2016; Acemoglu & Restrepo, 2019).

AI also facilitates human-machine collaboration in a variety of hybrid configurations. In areas such as medical diagnostics, financial advising, language translation, and customer service, AI systems are increasingly deployed as decision-support tools. Rather than replacing human judgment, these systems augment cognitive capacities by processing large volumes of data at high speed, identifying patterns, and suggesting actionable insights. For example, AI-assisted radiological tools can detect anomalies in medical imaging with high precision, but the final diagnosis still rests with the clinician, who interprets results in light of the patient's broader clinical context (Esteva et al., 2021; Rajpurkar et al., 2022).

This augmentation model presents a paradigm shift in the understanding of workplace automation. Instead of a binary distinction between tasks that are "automated" and those that are "not automatable," AI invites a rethinking of labor as a continuum of complementarity between human and machine capabilities. Workers become orchestrators of intelligent tools, whose effectiveness depends not only on algorithmic sophistication but also on human oversight, contextual understanding, and ethical deliberation. This shift has the potential to create new forms of value by enhancing service personalization, accelerating innovation cycles, and fostering cross-disciplinary collaboration (Brynjolfsson & McAfee, 2014; WEF, 2020).

However, realizing these opportunities requires deliberate organizational strategies that include employee training, participatory design, and a clear delineation of roles and responsibilities. The successful deployment of AI should not be evaluated solely in terms of technical performance or cost reduction, but also in terms of its ability to enhance human potential and contribute to a dignified and meaningful work experience.

3.2 Risks: Displacement, Wage Polarization, and Skill Mismatch

DESPITE THE POTENTIAL benefits associated with the integration of artificial intelligence (AI) into the workplace, concerns about job displacement remain at the forefront of public, academic, and policy discourse. In particular, occupations composed of highly codifiable, repetitive, or rule-based tasks are vulnerable to full or partial automation. Sectors such as retail, transportation, warehousing, and manufacturing have already witnessed substantial transformation due to the deployment of AI-enabled robotics, self-checkout systems, and autonomous vehicles (Frey & Osborne, 2017; Chui et al., 2018). These shifts threaten not only employment levels but also the occupational identities and economic stability of entire communities dependent on mid- and low-skilled labor.

One of the most pressing economic consequences of AI-induced automation is the risk of wage polarization. As demand for highly skilled professionals in areas such as data science, AI development, and system architecture increases, wages for these roles are expected to rise significantly. In contrast, many routine-intensive jobs in clerical support, logistics, and customer service are projected to decline in number and remuneration. This bifurcation of labor market outcomes contributes to a hollowing out of the middle-skill segment, reinforcing patterns of inequality that have deepened over the last several decades in advanced economies (Autor, 2015; Agrawal, Gans, & Goldfarb, 2019). Without compensatory mechanisms, such as progressive tax policy or robust labor protections, the economic benefits of AI risk becoming concentrated in elite segments of the workforce and corporate sector. Another structural concern relates to the evolving demand for skills. The introduction of AI reconfigures occupational structures and shifts the skillsets required to remain employable. Workers whose education or training does not align with AI-driven modes of production face a rapid devaluation of their competencies. The pace of this technological transformation may outstrip the ability of many workers—particularly older, low-income, or geographically immobile individuals—to adapt or retrain effectively (Brynjolfsson & McAfee, 2014; Autor et al., 2021). This skill mismatch can result in prolonged unemployment or underemployment, thereby exacerbating socioeconomic exclusion.

To mitigate these risks, sustained investment in lifelong learning, vocational retraining, and digital literacy is essential. Reskilling and upskilling programs should not be treated as peripheral interventions but rather as central pillars of economic resilience in the face of AI disruption. These programs must also be context-sensitive, addressing not only technical skills but also cognitive, social, and ethical competencies relevant to hybrid human–AI workplaces. Moreover, partnerships among governments, educational institutions, and industry actors are needed to align training with real labor market needs and ensure equitable access to new opportunities (World Economic Forum, 2020).

Ultimately, while the displacement effects of AI may vary by country, sector, and demographic group, the underlying pattern is clear: without proactive policy frameworks and inclusive institutional strategies, the diffusion of AI risks entrenching inequality and social fragmentation rather than fostering shared prosperity.

3.3 Complementarity versus Substitution: A Nuanced Perspective

THE IMPACT OF ARTIFICIAL intelligence (AI) on employment cannot be accurately captured through a binary lens of substitution versus preservation. A growing body of research emphasizes that most occupations are not wholly automatable; rather, they comprise a diverse set of tasks, only some of which are susceptible to automation. As such, the introduction of AI tends to transform jobs rather than eliminate them outright, prompting the emergence of new hybrid forms of work that integrate human judgment with machine precision (Brynjolfsson, Mitchell, & Rock, 2018). This paradigm of complementarity suggests that AI may function more as an augmentation technology than as a replacement. In practice, this entails machines taking on tasks characterized by scale, speed, and repetition—such as data processing, predictive modeling, or pattern recognition—while humans focus on responsibilities involving emotional intelligence, ethical judgment, creative reasoning, and interpersonal communication. For example, in clinical settings, AI algorithms may support physicians by flagging anomalies in medical scans, but the final diagnosis and treatment decisions remain dependent on the physician's interpretative and contextual expertise (Rajpurkar et al., 2022). Similarly, in the legal sector, natural language processing tools can assist with document review and case law retrieval, but they do not supplant the deliberative functions of legal reasoning or courtroom advocacy.

Empirical research supports this more granular task-based view. Autor and Handel (2013) argue that analyzing the impacts of automation at the occupational level conceals important variations in task content and the reorganization of responsibilities within jobs. A more precise evaluation requires shifting analytical focus to the task level, where the actual interface between human labor and machine capabilities is negotiated. This approach allows for greater specificity in identifying which components of a job are vulnerable to automation, which are enhanced by technology, and which remain distinctly human. Moreover, the coexistence of substitution and complementarity within the same job function or sector underscores the complexity of AI's labor market effects. Even when machines assume certain functions, new demands emerge for human oversight, interpretation, and supervision. These evolving dynamics highlight the necessity for workplace redesign and role redefinition, processes that are highly contingent on organizational strategy, sectoral characteristics, and institutional regulation (Holm & Lorenz, 2022). The recognition of AI as a transformative rather than purely disruptive force has important implications for policy and workforce development. It shifts the emphasis from protecting entire occupations to enabling workers to adapt to changing task compositions. This requires a coordinated strategy of task-level reskilling, continuous education, and participatory workplace innovation. It also demands that AI deployment be guided by design principles that promote meaningful human involvement, equity in task distribution, and value creation for all stakeholders. In this sense, the transition toward AI-enabled work is not predetermined by technical feasibility alone but is shaped by human choices—choices about how to organize labor, structure incentives, and define the role of machines in society.

3.4 Organizational Constraints and the Limits of Feasibility

ONE OF THE CRITICAL limitations in current automation risk assessments is their disproportionate focus on technical feasibility, often to the exclusion of contextual and organizational constraints. Many studies estimate automation potential by identifying tasks that can be performed by existing AI or robotic systems, thereby implying a linear trajectory from technical capability to actual adoption. However, as Holm and Lorenz (2022) argue, this assumption neglects the complex economic, institutional, and managerial realities that mediate technological diffusion.

The fact that a task is automatable in principle does not guarantee that it will be automated in practice. A wide range of non-technical factors influence whether AI is deployed within a given organization. These include financial constraints, the availability of digital infrastructure, the cost of data acquisition and integration, employee resistance, legal uncertainty, and the absence of a compelling business case. In some cases, the costs associated with AI implementation—ranging from capital expenditure to retraining programs and change management—may outweigh the projected gains in productivity or efficiency, especially for small and medium-sized enterprises (Chui et al., 2018; Bessen, 2019). Moreover, the reconfiguration of work processes to accommodate AI often necessitates substantial organizational redesign. This includes restructuring roles, reallocating tasks, and redefining performance metrics, all of which can disrupt established hierarchies and workflows. As a result, firms may adopt a cautious, incremental approach rather than pursuing large-scale automation, particularly when institutional inertia or strong labor protections are in place. Implementation feasibility is thus contingent not only on technological maturity but also on organizational readiness and adaptability.

Social acceptability further complicates AI deployment. The introduction of algorithmic systems into workplaces often raises ethical and psychological concerns among employees, including fears of job loss, deskilling, and increased surveillance. These perceptions can generate resistance, reduce morale, and undermine the legitimacy of technological change. In sectors such as healthcare and education, where trust, empathy, and interpersonal interaction are central to service delivery, the replacement of human judgment by machine output may face both cultural and professional opposition (Voss, 2021; ILO, 2023). Market structure and competitive dynamics also shape AI adoption. In highly commoditized sectors, firms may be under pressure to reduce labor costs through automation. In contrast, in markets where product differentiation relies on human-centric services—such as consulting, artisanal production, or high-end hospitality—the economic rationale for automation may be less compelling. In such cases, investments in AI may focus more on augmenting human labor rather than replacing it. A further consideration cuts across these constraints. The factors surveyed above are typically treated as frictions—delays between what is technically possible and what is actually deployed, to be overcome as costs fall and infrastructure matures. But the relation may be the reverse of what the friction metaphor suggests. Where predictive systems are integrated into the infrastructure through which decisions are executed rather than merely advised (Startari 2025b), the resulting arrangement is not slow to change but resistant to it: the categories, thresholds, and relative costs encoded at the moment of integration become the parameters within which subsequent decisions are made, and revising them requires an institutional act that the system's own operation does not provide for. What presents itself as delayed adoption may therefore be better understood as premature fixation. The question for automation assessment is not only how quickly a capability diffuses, but what it renders difficult to reconsider once it has.

Given these multifaceted constraints, automation risk assessments must go beyond task-level technical analyses and incorporate a broader understanding of implementation barriers. This includes evaluating organizational capacity, regulatory frameworks, sectoral characteristics, and cultural attitudes toward technology. Only by acknowledging these real-world frictions can we arrive at more accurate and actionable insights into the future of work in the age of AI.

3.5 Moving Toward a Strategic and Inclusive Transition

ADDRESSING THE MULTIFACETED challenges posed by artificial intelligence (AI) in the workplace necessitates coordinated action across multiple societal domains. The trajectory of AI integration is not predetermined by technical advancements alone, but is also shaped by public policy, institutional frameworks, and collective negotiation processes. Consequently, a strategic and inclusive transition toward AI-enabled labor markets requires deliberate efforts by governments, employers, trade unions, civil society, and educational institutions to co-design sustainable solutions.

Central to this process is the creation of robust vocational training and lifelong learning systems that enable workers to adapt to the evolving demands of the labor market. These programs should be tailored to the specific skills required in AI-augmented work environments, ranging from digital literacy and data management to critical thinking and interdisciplinary collaboration. Evidence from past industrial transformations suggests that investment in upskilling and reskilling can mitigate the negative effects of technological displacement, particularly when training is accessible, targeted, and aligned with regional labor market needs (Autor, Mindell, & Reynolds, 2021; OECD, 2024). In parallel, social protection mechanisms must be strengthened to provide income security, healthcare, and transitional support to workers who are displaced or at high risk of job loss due to automation. These mechanisms are essential not only for cushioning economic shocks but also for preserving social cohesion and democratic legitimacy during periods of technological upheaval. Without them, the risk of exclusion, marginalization, and political backlash may increase, undermining the social contract that sustains innovation (World Economic Forum, 2020; ILO, 2023). Equally important are regulatory frameworks that govern the use of AI in organizational and public contexts. As algorithmic decision-making becomes more prevalent in domains such as recruitment, credit scoring, and law enforcement, there is an urgent need to ensure that these systems are transparent, accountable, and non-discriminatory. Regulatory instruments should mandate explainability, establish redress mechanisms for affected individuals, and enforce compliance with ethical standards that reflect fundamental rights and democratic values (Floridi et al., 2018; Barocas, Hardt, & Narayanan, 2019). Furthermore, promoting human-centered AI design is a critical element of any inclusive strategy. This approach emphasizes the alignment of technological development with societal goals, prioritizing human autonomy, equity, and well-being over narrow efficiency metrics. By embedding participatory design practices and ethical impact assessments in the development lifecycle, AI technologies can be better adapted to diverse user needs and contexts of use (Doshi-Velez & Kim, 2017; Steijn, Luiijf, & van der Beek, 2016).

Ultimately, the success of the transition to an AI-integrated labor economy will depend not only on the technical capacity of machines but also on our collective ability to manage their deployment in a manner that maximizes opportunity while minimizing harm. Strategic governance, institutional trust, and inclusive policy design are the pillars upon which a just and sustainable AI transition must be built.

3.6 Rethinking Employment: From Substitution to Transformation

THE ASSESSMENT OF ARTIFICIAL intelligence's impact on employment and skills requires a nuanced and multidimensional approach. Contrary to deterministic models that assume a direct substitution of human labor by machines, current evidence increasingly suggests that AI adoption often entails a reconfiguration of tasks, rather than their outright elimination. Many occupations comprise a hybrid structure that includes both automatable components and inherently human functions such as creativity, ethical reasoning, emotional intelligence, and social interaction.

Traditional task-based frameworks, while useful, tend to understate the potential for augmentation and hybridization. In practice, AI systems are frequently deployed to support human decision-making in fields such as healthcare, logistics, customer service, education, and data analysis. In these contexts, machines process large volumes of information and generate probabilistic recommendations, but humans remain central in interpreting results, exercising judgment, and interacting with end users.

The effects of AI on the labor market cannot be decoupled from broader socio-economic dynamics, including technological diffusion rates, demographic trends, macroeconomic cycles, and institutional capacities. While certain jobs may be displaced, new occupations and industries are likely to emerge as AI systems enable novel forms of production and service delivery. These developments are expected to generate productivity gains, reduce operational costs, and enhance the competitiveness of firms, with possible positive repercussions for overall employment levels.

However, the realization of these potential benefits is not automatic. The distributional effects of AI may exacerbate existing inequalities unless adequate policy measures are implemented. Preparing the workforce for the evolving job landscape will require substantial investments in education and lifelong learning, particularly in digital literacy, problem-solving, and interdisciplinary competencies. Workers must be equipped not only to coexist with AI systems, but to thrive within human-machine collaborative environments.

Public policy has a critical role to play in mediating this transition. A proactive institutional framework should include well-designed reskilling programs, accessible income support mechanisms, and dynamic labor market regulations that foster mobility, security, and flexibility. In parallel, it is necessary to cultivate a culture of ethical AI deployment, ensuring that technological change serves inclusive and sustainable economic development.

In conclusion, the impact of AI on employment is neither linear nor uniform. It is shaped by a complex interplay of technological, organizational, and policy factors. Rather than focusing exclusively on risks of job elimination, it is more productive to explore how AI can transform the nature of work, enhance human capabilities, and stimulate economic renewal. The challenge for contemporary societies lies in managing this transformation deliberately, equitably, and intelligently—turning technological disruption into an opportunity for collective advancement.

CHAPTER 4: IMPACT OF WORK TRANSFORMATION: A SECTORAL PERSPECTIVE

The transformation of work driven by the adoption of artificial intelligence constitutes one of the most significant dynamics of the twenty-first century in the field of labor relations and productive organization. This chapter aims to examine, in depth and with scientific rigor, the current and potential impacts of artificial intelligence in the realm of work from a sectoral perspective. It begins with the premise, widely supported by contemporary literature, that the incorporation of intelligent systems into the labor environment is producing structural transformations that affect not only the skill sets required but also the material conditions of employment and the interaction between workers and their technological environments.

The central objective of this chapter is to analyze how artificial intelligence is being implemented in strategic sectors such as transportation, banking, and healthcare, and to rigorously evaluate the effects this technology is producing on the organization of labor, skill demands, occupational health and safety, and human relationships within the workplace. Based on a systematic review of the existing academic and technical literature, this chapter seeks to construct a comprehensive understanding of the transformations currently underway in diverse productive sectors. This review is complemented by the analysis of empirical studies and specific case examples in which AI is actively integrated into real-world work environments.

The analysis considers both the positive effects and the challenges associated with the adoption of artificial intelligence in professional settings. Among the aspects examined are the reconfiguration of skill requirements, the redistribution of tasks between human workers and automated systems, the automation of operational processes, the quality of employment resulting from these changes, emergent occupational risks, and the transformation of interpersonal and machine-mediated interactions in the workplace. The purpose is not merely to describe the changes observed but to understand their scope and structural implications.

To ensure the validity and precision of its findings, this chapter employs a rigorous methodological approach that combines quantitative and qualitative data analysis, the study of AI systems applied to labor contexts, and consultation with experts and researchers specialized in artificial intelligence and labor organization. It also includes a critical review of the methodologies employed in the analyzed studies, identifying potential biases, methodological limitations, and analytical gaps, particularly in relation to how the real impact of artificial intelligence on work transformation is assessed. This approach makes it possible to distinguish between generalizable impacts and those that are specific to each sector, taking into account that the capacity to implement intelligent systems, their integration into work processes, and their consequences for the workforce vary significantly depending on the type of activity, organizational structure, regulatory environment, and digital maturity of each industry.

Finally, the chapter presents evidence-based recommendations for the development of future research, as well as for the formulation of public policy and corporate strategy that can responsibly and sustainably accompany the transformation of work. It is grounded in the conviction that a deep, sectorally differentiated, and academically informed understanding of the effects of artificial intelligence on labor is essential for sound decision-making in labor policy, talent formation, and strategic planning in an increasingly automated and digitized environment.

4.1 Artificial Intelligence in the Healthcare Sector

THE INTEGRATION OF artificial intelligence in the healthcare sector has generated intense interest in recent years, not only for its potential to optimize clinical processes but also for the fundamental ethical and structural questions it raises. Healthcare is a sector defined by its intensive reliance on knowledge, constant innovation in medical technologies and treatments, and high-volume data generation across institutional, clinical, and patient-level domains. These characteristics make the sector particularly fertile ground for the application of AI, especially when intelligent systems are trained to identify patterns in complex medical datasets and support evidence-based decision-making processes.

Artificial intelligence offers a range of possibilities to enhance diagnostic accuracy, predict treatment outcomes, allocate resources more efficiently, and support public health monitoring and planning. Its potential to transform health systems, however, is conditioned by the quality of the data employed, the interpretability of algorithms, and the ethical frameworks within which these technologies are implemented. The scale of healthcare-related data is unprecedented: electronic health records, imaging systems, genomics, wearable devices, and health apps generate vast quantities of information daily. According to recent estimates, the global healthcare data volume is expected to reach 50 zettabytes by 2025, doubling approximately every 73 days (IDC, 2023). The ability to process this data intelligently and securely is emerging as a critical determinant of national health system performance.

Economically, the healthcare sector represents one of the most significant components of global expenditure. According to the World Bank and OECD data from 2024, healthcare spending accounts for approximately 10.6 percent of global GDP and exceeds that threshold in many countries, including the United States (17.8%), Germany

(12.7%), France (12.3%), the United Kingdom (11.9%), and Brazil (9.5%). This sustained investment reflects demographic transitions—such as population aging—and epidemiological changes, including the rising prevalence of chronic non-communicable diseases, multimorbidity, and mental health disorders. While healthcare systems are under pressure to expand access and improve quality, public budgets remain under severe constraint. The OECD (2024) estimates that at least 20 percent of healthcare spending yields no measurable improvement in health outcomes and may even contribute to overtreatment or harm. These inefficiencies have made the healthcare sector a prime target for innovation initiatives from both traditional health institutions and major technology firms. Companies such as Google (through DeepMind and Google Health), Amazon (via Amazon Clinic and AWS HealthLake), Apple (with HealthKit and wearable integration), Microsoft (with Azure AI for Healthcare), and Meta (in partnership with medical imaging initiatives) are increasingly investing in healthcare platforms and services. These actors are introducing AI-driven tools that offer diagnostic support, optimize medical workflows, or enhance patient engagement. Their growing influence underscores the need for careful analysis of both the benefits and systemic risks associated with integrating private AI technologies into public health infrastructures.

Healthcare is not a homogeneous domain. It encompasses a wide range of professions and competencies, from highly specialized disciplines such as neurosurgery and oncology to the complex relational work of nurses, case managers, caregivers, and public health coordinators. The diversity of roles implies multiple points of contact with artificial intelligence systems, whether through automated triage platforms, clinical decision support systems, robotic surgery, AI-enabled diagnostic imaging, or patient monitoring systems. Labor costs constitute a substantial proportion of healthcare budgets, and the possibility of substituting some tasks performed by human workers with intelligent machines has been widely discussed in both academic literature and institutional reports.

AI systems currently perform well in narrow domains characterized by well-defined problems and structured data. For example, convolutional neural networks have demonstrated expert-level performance in fracture detection from radiological images, melanoma identification from dermoscopic photographs, and tumor segmentation in oncology (Esteva et al., 2021; Rajpurkar et al., 2022). These applications often rely on established clinical guidelines and focus on single-pathology scenarios. However, real-world medicine increasingly involves patients with multiple comorbidities and interacting chronic conditions, a context that challenges current AI capacities and reveals their epistemological and practical limitations.

Managing complex multimorbidity, particularly among aging populations, is likely to become a central challenge for health systems worldwide in the coming decades. The shift from acute, episodic care to long-term, coordinated, and preventive care demands more than algorithmic precision. It requires interdisciplinary collaboration, integration across medical and social services, and sensitivity to patients' psychological and behavioral contexts. AI tools designed without consideration for this complexity risk reinforcing reductive models of care and neglecting essential human dimensions. The future of effective healthcare, therefore, lies in the integration of AI not as a replacement for human expertise, but as a complementary tool that enhances systemic capacity while preserving the relational and ethical foundations of medicine. The effectiveness of artificial intelligence in disease detection cannot be reduced merely to the volume of data available. The quality of a medical diagnosis depends not only on the quantity of information collected but also on the capacity to interpret complex and dynamic phenomena that are not governed by fixed or deterministic rules. Unlike closed systems where AI can achieve high predictive accuracy based on regularities in data, the human body and its interaction with socio-environmental factors present non-linear and contingent characteristics that limit the generalizability of algorithmic solutions. Medical knowledge, particularly in cases involving multimorbidity, mental health, or psychosomatic disorders, requires interpretive reasoning, clinical judgment, and contextual awareness—capacities that are not reproducible by current AI systems.

The dynamic nature of human life, the uniqueness of each clinical case, and the unpredictability of many health outcomes imply that full automation in medical decision-making is neither desirable nor viable. Human beings possess adaptive capacities that allow them to respond to novel and unexpected situations, negotiate meaning with patients, and adjust behavior according to non-programmed feedback. These forms of practical and ethical reasoning cannot be autonomously replicated by artificial intelligence, regardless of data scale or algorithmic complexity. Furthermore, issues of responsibility and accountability in healthcare are fundamentally different from those in other automated environments. Misdiagnosis or inappropriate treatment, even if statistically rare, may result in severe consequences, including permanent disability or death. This introduces ethical and legal considerations that go beyond technical performance and concern the legitimacy of delegation to AI in life-critical scenarios.

Therefore, while artificial intelligence can serve as a valuable complementary tool in healthcare, its capacity to substitute clinical professionals is limited and should be rigorously examined. The deployment of AI in this sector must be guided by principles of proportionality, transparency, explainability, and shared responsibility, especially when its use affects vulnerable populations or decision-making under uncertainty. A comprehensive evaluation of its impact requires integrating not only accuracy and efficiency metrics but also human-centered criteria such as empathy, trust, and communicative efficacy.

More broadly, artificial intelligence invites a systemic rethinking of how healthcare is conceptualized and organized. Historically, health systems in industrialized countries were structured around acute and episodic care models, focused on well-defined pathologies such as fractures, infections, or tumors. In such settings, which operate according to linear diagnostic and therapeutic protocols, AI systems can introduce efficiencies that resemble those found in industrial production models. However, the future of medicine is likely to shift toward the long-term management of complex, chronic, and poly-pathological conditions, where psychological, behavioral, and social factors play a crucial role. Addressing obesity, diabetes, addiction, and mental health disorders, for example, requires sustained engagement, behavior modification, and patient empowerment.

In this context, AI may help identify risk profiles, anticipate relapses, or optimize treatment pathways, but it cannot replace the human relationship that underlies motivational interviewing, therapeutic alliance, or ethical counseling. Case studies such as Kaiser Permanente Washington illustrate how AI-based systems can be successfully integrated with interdisciplinary teams of clinicians, nurses, health coaches, and community workers to improve prevention and care for multifactorial diseases. These experiences support the hypothesis that rather than reducing the need for healthcare professionals, AI may increase the demand for relational and coordination-intensive roles. Moreover, AI may contribute to the emergence of new healthcare professions and the transformation of existing ones. As digital health ecosystems expand, roles such as data health analysts, AI-augmented clinicians, clinical algorithm auditors, and virtual care coordinators are likely to become essential components of healthcare teams. The work of highly specialized professionals, such as oncologists or cardiologists, may evolve to include oversight of algorithmic recommendations and the integration of real-time data streams into decision-making. Likewise, frontline workers such as nurses and care assistants may increasingly rely on AI tools for personalized monitoring and early warning systems, especially in remote or home-care settings.

Remote patient monitoring systems supported by AI could facilitate personalized responses tailored to individual contexts, drawing upon clinical records, social determinants of health, and behavioral history. AI could also play a role in hospital admission processes by pre-analyzing medical histories and suggesting care strategies, improving communication between services and streamlining coordination across different care levels. These transformations would not eliminate traditional nursing functions, but rather reshape their modalities of intervention, requiring enhanced digital literacy and interprofessional collaboration.

Ultimately, the integration of artificial intelligence in healthcare must be evaluated not only through economic or technological metrics but also through its effects on professional identity, patient autonomy, and the organization of care. This requires a governance framework that aligns innovation with public values and ensures that technological change reinforces, rather than weakens, the humanistic foundations of medicine.

The integration of artificial intelligence in healthcare also presents opportunities to improve the internal organization of work and alleviate pressure on clinical and administrative personnel. One significant contribution of AI systems lies in their capacity to enhance the coordination of actions among healthcare professionals, which is critical for quality care delivery. By enabling real-time data sharing, streamlining communication, and facilitating cross-functional planning, AI systems can reduce fragmentation and promote integrated care pathways. This, in turn, may improve both clinical outcomes and workplace satisfaction.

Organizational efficiency remains a pressing issue in healthcare. According to data from the OECD, approximately 20 percent of healthcare spending in member countries is wasted due to inefficiencies in care delivery, poor coordination, and excessive administrative burdens (OECD, 2017; OECD, 2024). AI applications that support hospital activity coding, diagnostic planning, triage, and patient prioritization can contribute to optimizing resource allocation. By anticipating patient flows and improving capacity management, AI can help hospitals adjust staffing, reduce bottlenecks, and allocate resources more precisely. These improvements lighten the administrative workload of healthcare professionals, allowing more time for patient interaction and reducing job stress.

This reduction in bureaucratic pressure is particularly important in an environment where many hospitals face systemic challenges such as understaffing, excessive workload, and increasing case complexity. AI systems that automate repetitive tasks—such as scheduling, documentation, or inventory management—can improve the working conditions of overburdened clinical teams, mitigating the physical and psychological exhaustion often associated with emergency and chronic care. However, this transformation also raises concerns regarding employment in non-medical support roles. According to public health policy expert David Gruson, up to 15 percent of administrative and logistical positions in hospitals—such as those related to reception, patient transport coordination, and resource management—could be made redundant by AI-based automation (Gruson, 2019). These effects are expected to intensify as AI tools become more sophisticated, generating tension between the goals of efficiency and employment stability. A balanced approach to AI adoption must therefore consider not only technical performance but also social impacts, requiring institutional mechanisms to support professional reconversion and role evolution.

In addition to administrative restructuring, AI is increasingly being tested in psychosocial interventions, particularly in geriatrics and long-term care. The management of patients with chronic neurodegenerative conditions, such as Alzheimer's disease, presents a major organizational and ethical challenge. These patients frequently suffer from behavioral symptoms—anxiety, aggression, wandering, or apathy—that are difficult to manage and place a significant emotional and logistical burden on healthcare teams. Due to communication difficulties and emotional distress, many patients experience isolation, which exacerbates both clinical outcomes and caregiver stress. The accumulation of such stress factors often leads to burnout among healthcare professionals, as well as excessive reliance on pharmacological treatments such as psychotropic medications.

In response to these challenges, several initiatives have explored the use of AI-assisted robotic systems to mediate patient-caregiver interactions. One notable case is the implementation of Paro, an interactive robot designed to engage older patients through auditory, tactile, and emotional responses. In a study conducted in a hospital geriatric unit, 100 percent of surveyed staff acknowledged lacking effective tools to manage complex cases involving behavioral disorders. Following the introduction of Paro, participants reported reduced levels of patient anxiety, improved mood, and lower usage of sedative medications (Demange et al., 2019). These results were corroborated by international studies, which found that robotic companions not only improved patients' well-being but also had a positive effect on staff morale and task management.

While such technologies are not substitutes for human care, they demonstrate how AI-mediated interventions can enhance patient outcomes and improve workplace dynamics when implemented thoughtfully and ethically. Their success depends on user acceptance, integration into care protocols, and rigorous evaluation, as well as continuous collaboration between engineers, clinicians, and caregivers.

4.2 Artificial Intelligence in the Transportation Sector

THE TRANSPORTATION sector has emerged as one of the principal frontiers for the implementation of artificial intelligence, particularly through the development of autonomous vehicles and AI-based logistics systems. The magnitude of this transformation will depend on the level of automation achieved and the speed at which various technologies diffuse across modes of transport. Although the promise of fully autonomous vehicles has long occupied a central place in technological forecasts, the concrete deployment of such systems remains limited and uneven.

A central concept in assessing this transformation is the SAE International classification system, which defines six levels of vehicle automation, from Level 0 (no automation) to Level 5 (full autonomy in all environments). As of 2025, no manufacturer has yet announced a commercially available Level 5 vehicle. Experiments in driverless navigation began in the late 2010s, led by firms such as Waymo in the United States and Navya in France. Nonetheless, full autonomy across all road conditions remains a long-term goal. According to John Krafcik, former CEO of Waymo, the realization of Level 5 autonomy may take several decades, and even then, autonomous vehicles may still require human supervision in exceptional conditions (Krafcik, 2021).

In the foreseeable future, the most significant progress is expected to occur at Level 4, where vehicles can operate autonomously in constrained and predictable environments such as highways, parking lots, or dedicated urban corridors. Within the next five to ten years, these systems may begin to alter labor structures in sectors such as road transport and rail operations, especially where long-distance freight and regularized transport routes facilitate technical feasibility. Consequently, the analysis of AI's impact in this chapter will focus on the likely diffusion of Level 4 automation and its implications for the organization of labor, employment dynamics, and productivity across ground transport industries.

The development of autonomous trucks represents a particularly salient case. Road freight transport, which accounts for a substantial proportion of logistical movement in North America and Europe, is considered a promising area for full automation due to the standardized nature of long-distance highway routes and the economic incentives to reduce labor costs. The automation of freight vehicles may allow companies to bypass regulatory constraints related to mandatory rest periods, operate in continuous platoons to reduce fuel consumption, and optimize fleet management through enhanced flexibility. These changes could generate significant productivity gains while helping to address the persistent shortage of professional drivers observed in several countries.

However, the full integration of autonomous trucks into commercial operations depends on regulatory harmonization, industry standards, and the development of secure and interoperable digital infrastructures. According to a survey conducted by the International Transport Forum, more than half of transportation experts anticipate that vehicle platooning will become widespread by 2030, whereas fully autonomous freight operations may not be commercially viable before 2050. Pilot projects in ports, mining facilities, and controlled environments have demonstrated the potential of these technologies, but no commercial deployment of Level 4 or Level 5 autonomous freight vehicles has been recorded as of early 2025. Existing tests involve onboard human supervision, reflecting continued technical, legal, and ethical constraints.

In addition to vehicle automation, AI is increasingly applied in logistics, infrastructure management, and predictive maintenance. The proliferation of industrial sensors has enabled the large-scale collection of real-time operational data from vehicles, transport systems, and physical infrastructure. AI algorithms can process this data at a speed and scale far beyond human capabilities, allowing for the development of intelligent diagnostic systems. These tools can detect signs of mechanical wear, analyze operating patterns, and anticipate anomalies, thereby enabling predictive rather than preventive maintenance protocols. This approach reduces unplanned downtimes, extends the life of critical equipment, and optimizes resource allocation in maintenance departments.

These developments are particularly relevant for rail networks, which operate under high-capacity constraints and complex scheduling systems. AI-based systems can dynamically reconfigure transport flows in response to disruptions, managing variables such as train availability, track usage, passenger demand, and emergency scenarios. In cases of breakdown or congestion, AI systems can assess the optimal speed to alleviate bottlenecks, deploy replacement units based on workforce availability, and propose alternative routing strategies. Such systems rely on the real-time integration of diverse data sources, including traffic patterns, meteorological conditions, and passenger behavior, which poses significant challenges in terms of data governance and inter-organizational coordination.

In this regard, logistical optimization through AI is not limited to cost-efficiency. It also introduces the possibility of improving service continuity, reducing environmental impact, and enhancing passenger safety. However, these benefits come with structural challenges related to labor substitution, new occupational risks associated with automated systems, and potential cyber vulnerabilities in interconnected infrastructures. The expansion of AI in transport must therefore be accompanied by robust regulatory frameworks that address not only technological reliability, but also employment protection, liability allocation, and cross-border interoperability.

The social consequences of automation in transport also deserve critical attention. In scenarios of partial automation, existing workers may experience task restructuring, reduced autonomy, or surveillance-based performance monitoring. In fully automated contexts, entire job categories—particularly those involving routine driving tasks—may become obsolete. However, as with other sectors, AI may also create new roles in maintenance analytics, remote operations, cybersecurity, and systems supervision. The net impact on employment will depend not only on the pace of technological change, but also on policy responses and the capacity to design inclusive transitions that prioritize human dignity, retraining, and equity.

The technological applications associated with artificial intelligence in the transportation sector are progressively reaching a level of maturity that could allow for widespread implementation over the next five to ten years. However, this maturity cannot be assessed solely in terms of algorithmic performance or mechanical feasibility. The successful deployment of autonomous systems also depends on data availability at scale, the resolution of privacy issues related to connected vehicles, and the establishment of clear economic and institutional frameworks for data exchange. The operation of autonomous vehicles requires real-time access to massive datasets concerning vehicle performance, infrastructure conditions, navigation environments, and traffic dynamics. These data flows must be harmonized across actors such as road and rail infrastructure managers, vehicle manufacturers, logistics firms, and public authorities. In this regard, the central challenge is not merely technical but economic and political. Issues surrounding data ownership, interoperability, and distribution of value among stakeholders will play a decisive role in determining how effectively AI technologies are integrated into transport systems. The creation of open and standardized platforms for data sharing—particularly for navigation, diagnostics, and predictive maintenance—will be essential. Without coordinated policy action, fragmentation and data silos may impede the full realization of AI's potential in improving safety, efficiency, and responsiveness in transportation networks.

The impact of AI on occupations and skill profiles within the transportation sector is most visible in the case of road freight transport. Driving remains a core function in this domain, and the development of autonomous trucks could fundamentally alter the demand for labor. If Level 4 vehicles capable of operating autonomously on highways become operational within a ten-year horizon, the role of professional drivers is likely to be redefined. In certain corridors or operational contexts, automation could reduce the need for long-haul drivers by enabling continuous operation beyond human working-hour limits. This, in turn, may lead to a contraction in demand for long-distance trucking labor, particularly in countries where freight transport depends heavily on interstate highway systems.

However, the transition will not be immediate or homogeneous. The implementation of autonomous freight vehicles presupposes a robust regulatory architecture, standardization of safety protocols, and resolution of legal ambiguities surrounding liability and accident response. Moreover, certain tasks in the transport chain—such as loading, unloading, refueling, and customer interaction—remain non-automated and continue to require human labor. In many cases, autonomous trucks will require a hybrid model in which human drivers take control in non-highway segments or provide supervision and logistical support. Additionally, the diffusion of AI systems is likely to generate new roles and skill demands. The operation and monitoring of autonomous fleets will create demand for control-center personnel tasked with supervising real-time vehicle performance, responding to alerts, and managing fleet coordination. These workers will need technical expertise in areas such as data systems, network security, remote diagnostics, and human-machine interaction. The skills required for these emerging roles are distinct from those traditionally associated with commercial driving, highlighting the need for proactive workforce development strategies.

The transformation of the truck driving profession also involves profound implications for occupational identity, regulation, and labor protections. Historically, truck driving has been a central employment pathway for working-class men in many economies, particularly in rural or peri-urban regions. The erosion of this occupation due to automation could contribute to economic dislocation and social polarization if appropriate compensatory measures are not implemented. At the same time, new opportunities may arise for drivers in last-mile logistics, fleet support services, and regional delivery systems, especially in contexts where full automation is not technically feasible or economically justified.

The supervision and remote control of automated fleets may become a new employment niche, combining operational oversight with decision-making support in complex or unforeseen scenarios. These functions will require not only technical skills but also competencies related to ethical judgment, incident management, and the interpretation of AI-generated alerts or anomalies. The redistribution of tasks may therefore redefine the nature of labor in transport from physical operation toward systemic coordination and digital supervision.

It is important to emphasize that employment projections in this sector remain speculative and contingent on numerous factors, including technological progress, policy interventions, consumer behavior, and macroeconomic trends. Nonetheless, the transformative potential of AI in the transport sector requires that governments and industries prepare for non-linear labor transitions. Strategies for fair transition and retraining will be critical to ensure that the benefits of automation do not come at the cost of social cohesion and human security. Workforce development policies should not only focus on technical skills, but also promote adaptive capacities, cross-functional training, and ethical awareness in the context of human-AI collaboration.

The emergence of Level 4 autonomous vehicles in public transportation introduces new opportunities not only in terms of technological innovation but also in the configuration of services and labor dynamics. While these vehicles are unlikely to substantially impact the private use of automobiles in the short term, their deployment in public and semi-public transit systems may alter mobility patterns. Pilot programs for autonomous shuttles are currently underway in various regions, particularly in low-density urban areas or closed environments such as business campuses, airports, and university grounds. Companies such as Navya have deployed over fifty autonomous units worldwide, suggesting the beginning of a transition toward localized, AI-enabled mobility services.

These autonomous shuttles are designed to operate on predefined routes and offer potential value in covering "last mile" journeys or off-peak routes that are underserved by conventional mass transit. In doing so, they may reduce dependency on private vehicles for short distances and provide a viable alternative to ride-hailing services during hours when traditional public transport is unavailable. Nevertheless, due to infrastructure limitations and traffic saturation risks, these vehicles are unlikely to replace high-capacity public transport on congested corridors in the near future. Until fully autonomous driving (Level 5) is achieved—something not projected to be viable before 2040—taxis and app-based ride services will remain the dominant mode for flexible, door-to-door travel.

In parallel with this deployment, job creation is anticipated in areas related to fleet supervision, customer service, safety assurance, and technical support. These roles will require competencies in digital coordination, service logistics, and real-time incident management. The success of these autonomous systems will depend not only on their engineering, but on their social integration and operational reliability in complex urban environments.

The shift toward intelligent and connected vehicles is also expected to transform the roles and required skills of maintenance personnel. AI-powered diagnostic tools are increasingly embedded into new vehicles and retrofitted into existing fleets. These tools can generate precise fault detection, maintenance forecasts, and prescriptive repair instructions. In the context of predictive maintenance, the system may diagnose the fault, suggest the timing of the intervention, and propose the repair strategy, reducing uncertainty and reactive interventions.

However, this efficiency entails the risk of functional deskilling. As AI systems assume diagnostic functions, maintenance technicians may gradually lose a holistic understanding of vehicle systems, becoming reliant on algorithmic outputs. This parallel concerns in other domains, such as medicine, where algorithmic diagnostics may erode clinical reasoning if used uncritically. Preserving broad operational knowledge in maintenance occupations thus becomes a pedagogical and organizational challenge. Rather than reducing human autonomy to task execution, training programs should aim to balance specialization with systemic comprehension, enabling workers to intervene when intelligent tools fail or produce ambiguous results.

Predictive maintenance can also optimize the workflow of maintenance centers, allowing for more accurate forecasting of service demand, reducing overload during peak periods, and improving inventory and workforce planning. Nonetheless, its implementation must be accompanied by deliberate skill development strategies that uphold workforce autonomy and sustain the epistemic integrity of maintenance work.

4.3 Artificial Intelligence in the Banking and Financial Sector

THE BANKING SECTOR has been a pioneer in the adoption of digital technologies and automated systems, making it one of the most advanced environments for artificial intelligence applications. Due to the highly structured nature of financial data and the digitalization of core banking operations, the sector offers a fertile testing ground for AI systems in functions ranging from customer service to compliance, risk modeling, and asset management.

In the domain of customer relationship management, AI is most prominently used in credit scoring and risk assessment. Traditional statistical models have been employed for decades to estimate the probability of default among borrowers. More recently, these models have been supplemented by machine learning algorithms that incorporate non-traditional variables and extract predictive patterns from large datasets. This shift allows for more granular risk stratification but raises questions regarding data fairness, transparency, and explainability, particularly when AI models draw on behavioral or third-party data with potential bias.

Conversational AI systems, particularly chatbots and virtual assistants, represent one of the most visible and transformative aspects of AI deployment in banking. These systems allow for 24/7 interaction with customers, addressing basic queries, initiating transactions, and redirecting complex cases to human agents. The incorporation of natural language processing has significantly enhanced their performance and user experience. According to Satheesh et al. (2018), conversational agents are reshaping the nature of client-facing work, reducing the number of routine interactions handled by front-office staff and allowing human employees to focus on higher-value, personalized services.

AI is also playing a growing role in financial operations and asset management. In portfolio management, AI tools are used to analyze weak signals in financial markets, detect emerging trends, and generate real-time investment recommendations. These applications are increasingly important in high-frequency trading and algorithmic fund management, where millisecond-level decisions influence market outcomes. Furthermore, AI systems are being used to optimize capital allocation and model macroeconomic scenarios for institutional investors.

In the domain of compliance and regulation, AI has been deployed to detect anomalous transactions, identify potential cases of fraud, and support anti-money laundering (AML) efforts. Algorithms trained on transaction patterns, geographic data, and historical risk profiles can flag suspicious activity with increasing accuracy. Optical character recognition and image analysis systems are also used to automate customer identity verification, extracting and processing data from scanned ID documents.

These innovations are reshaping the occupational landscape of banking. While certain administrative and clerical roles may decline, there is a growing demand for data scientists, algorithm auditors, AI ethics officers, and specialists in financial cybersecurity. The success of AI adoption in the banking sector will depend on how institutions balance automation with human oversight, preserve client trust, and ensure that innovation aligns with evolving regulatory standards.

The progressive implementation of artificial intelligence in the banking sector is redefining both the structure of labor and the competencies required across multiple operational layers. According to Athling (2017), the profession of the banking advisor is undergoing a transformation that affects not only technical and compliance-related responsibilities, but also the very identity of client relationship roles. Tasks related to regulatory monitoring, fiscal oversight, and risk detection—including money laundering and tax fraud—are increasingly performed or augmented by intelligent systems. Tools such as Doctrine, a legal search engine powered by AI, illustrate the growing role of algorithmic assistance in navigating complex regulatory frameworks.

This transformation is occurring in tandem with shifting consumer expectations, particularly the demand for uninterrupted, omnichannel service. As banks transition toward 24/7 availability, a hybrid model of automated and human support is emerging. Under this model, AI systems triage requests and resolve common queries, while more complex interactions are managed by human agents. In some cases, a two-tiered service model is envisioned, where basic AI assistance is offered at no cost, and personalized human service is reserved for premium clients or specific use cases. This could result in a bifurcation of platform operation roles: a reduction in the number of frontline workers for routine inquiries, combined with an increase in the complexity and cognitive demands of the remaining roles.

The increasing effectiveness of AI in resolving platform-related questions, especially concerning online banking—now the primary interaction channel for most customers—has the potential to offload substantial administrative work. This reallocation of tasks may enable banks to train service agents to handle functions traditionally assigned to advisors, thereby reshaping internal role hierarchies. Customers now increasingly perceive their advisor not as a co-manager of their financial portfolio, but as a support interface capable of resolving a broad array of issues on demand.

In this evolving environment, new actors are emerging. Integrated service providers specializing in customer relations and data aggregation—often operating for third parties—are leveraging AI to offer entirely automated support systems. The concept of "bot-shoring" replaces traditional offshoring: instead of relocating services abroad to reduce labor costs, companies now assess which processes can be automated locally, minimizing expenses without geographic displacement. This shift further intensifies competition in the sector, pressuring traditional banks to accelerate their digital transformation strategies.

Paradoxically, AI can also reinforce the value of human advisors by automating low-value tasks and enabling them to focus on personalized consultation. As AI reduces the cognitive burden of regulatory or procedural tasks, advisors may devote more attention to understanding client goals, recommending financial products, and providing strategic guidance. This transition would prioritize relational and decision-making skills, encouraging financial institutions to invest in training programs focused on negotiation, communication, and personalized advising. Whether AI in banking leads to further digitization or rehumanization of financial services depends largely on the strategic decisions taken by institutional leaders.

Beyond client-facing roles, the implementation of AI in support functions is accelerating. Tasks involving data collection, information validation, and transaction monitoring are increasingly subject to optimization or automation. While AI does not radically restructure information systems, it extends existing trends initiated with robotic process automation (RPA) during the 1990s. In compliance-related domains, AI applications can enhance competencies such as responsiveness and adaptability, and reinforce digital and office-related skills. These areas, in turn, are linked to higher employability, suggesting that AI-induced transformations may not necessarily result in job losses but rather in job requalification.

The sectoral prospective analysis conducted by international organizations such as the Economic Commission for Latin America and the Caribbean (CEPAL) reveals the heterogeneous and multidimensional nature of AI's impact. Transformations induced by AI affect tasks, professions, work organization, and labor relations. Three types of tasks can be identified. First, there are novel tasks enabled by AI, such as continuous monitoring through connected devices in healthcare. Second, there is the automation of previously manual operations, such as autonomous road freight driving or automated fraud detection in banking. These transformations tend to devalue certain procedural competencies, such as routine planning or regulatory compliance, now ensured by algorithmic systems. Third, there are tasks that continue to require human intervention due to the current limits of AI, such as complex medical care or driving in highly variable traffic conditions.

Importantly, the deployment of AI not only transforms existing jobs but generates new professions related to the design, implementation, monitoring, and maintenance of intelligent systems. These roles encompass a wide spectrum of qualifications. At the high end, AI researchers and data scientists are essential to model development and system architecture. However, other functions—such as training data supervision, error correction, algorithm evaluation, and field testing—require medium or low levels of specialization. Although these roles may not constitute a majority of employment, they are crucial for ensuring the functionality, safety, and accountability of AI systems.

To meet the demand for such roles, education and certification programs in AI-related disciplines are proliferating worldwide. Institutions have begun to offer specialized degrees in data engineering, ethical AI management, algorithm auditing, and applied machine learning. The emergence of these professions suggests that the long-term impact of AI on employment in banking and finance will be not merely one of reduction or substitution, but rather recomposition and diversification, with qualitative shifts in knowledge requirements and labor structures.

4.4 Sectoral Impacts of Artificial Intelligence: Transformations, Tensions, and the Future of Work

THE ANALYSIS OF ARTIFICIAL intelligence (AI) across three core economic sectors—healthcare, transportation, and banking—reveals both the heterogeneity and the structural depth of the transformations currently underway. Far from producing uniform effects, AI alters occupational landscapes according to the nature of tasks, the regulatory frameworks, and the strategic choices adopted by organizations. It reorganizes labor processes, modifies skill hierarchies, and redefines the distribution of responsibilities between humans and intelligent systems.

Among the most salient findings is the potential of AI to foster continuous learning and improve organizational performance when deployed in collaborative human-machine environments. In healthcare, AI has supported diagnostic accuracy and enabled new forms of patient monitoring; in transportation, it has introduced predictive maintenance systems and initiated the gradual shift toward automation of mobility; in banking, it has restructured customer interaction and risk modeling. In all cases, AI has liberated workers from repetitive, routine tasks and opened space for more complex, analytical, or interpersonal functions.

This transformation brings to the fore the valorization of social and human skills. As AI systems assume operational and computational roles, human competencies such as empathy, negotiation, ethical reasoning, and contextual interpretation gain prominence. In professions historically underappreciated—such as healthcare assistants, customer service agents, and logistics coordinators—interpersonal and adaptive capacities now constitute key contributions to performance. More broadly, AI strengthens all professions that rely on human interaction, trust-building, and discretion.

Yet this shift is not without tensions or contradictions. The delegation of tasks to AI systems may also lead to increased cognitive workload for workers, particularly as tasks become more complex and high-stakes. Freed from mechanical duties, employees are now expected to interpret machine outputs, evaluate algorithmic suggestions, and assume final responsibility for decisions whose inner logic may be opaque. The case of diagnostic AI in medicine or predictive algorithms in vehicle maintenance illustrates the difficulty of maintaining accountability in the face of technological opacity. In the context of deep learning, where model interpretability is limited, the necessity for critical reflection, verification, and justification becomes even more acute. These changes also pose challenges to cognitive integrity. As some functions are automated, the skills they once required may atrophy through disuse. The example of GPS navigation and its documented impact on spatial orientation capacities is emblematic of this risk. Organizations and developers must therefore confront the question of which human abilities should be preserved, and how AI systems might be designed to support, rather than replace, cognitive engagement. Designing for symbiosis rather than substitution requires governance principles that protect human flourishing as a central value.

The effects of AI on work also depend on the strategic orientation of each institution. When AI is deployed to enhance the quality of work and encourage autonomy, it can yield substantial benefits in motivation, learning, and organizational performance. Conversely, when its introduction is guided primarily by cost-cutting imperatives, AI may restrict learning dynamics, undermine professional discretion, and exacerbate inequalities. In this regard, the business model and institutional culture of the adopting organization play a pivotal role in shaping outcomes.

Finally, the chapter underscores the importance of sector-specific regulation and governance frameworks. The risks of cognitive overload, skill degradation, and work-related stress associated with AI integration require structured responses. Emerging research, such as surveys conducted in Japan, suggest that although workers report satisfaction in performing more intellectually demanding tasks facilitated by AI, they also experience increased stress and uncertainty. These findings invite the implementation of normative instruments that ensure a fair and sustainable distribution of cognitive labor within AI-augmented environments. In conclusion, the sectoral analysis of AI reveals a dynamic and non-linear transformation of work. It is not automation per se, but the logic of implementation and the governance of its effects that will determine whether AI will contribute to human development or reinforce mechanistic models of labor. The future of work will depend on how societies, institutions, and individuals negotiate the balance between efficiency and dignity, between intelligent systems and meaningful human agency.

4.5 Human–Machine Collaboration and Emerging Workplace Risks

THE INTEGRATION OF AI-based robotic systems into human labor environments has expanded considerably in recent years, particularly through the adoption of collaborative robots, or *cobots*. These systems, designed to operate in proximity to human workers, are increasingly used in sectors such as industrial manufacturing, logistics, warehouse automation, and even healthcare. Their primary functions include supporting heavy load transport, assisting in assembly line operations via robotic arms or exoskeletons, and autonomously navigating factory or hospital corridors. By combining precise, repetitive motion with ergonomic assistance, cobots aim to reduce physical strain, mitigate workplace injuries, and extend the working capabilities of aging or disabled employees.

In principle, the use of cobots can contribute positively to occupational health by reducing biomechanical risks. Tasks involving repetitive strain, forced posture, or excessive load handling—recognized risk factors for musculoskeletal disorders—can be partially automated or shared between humans and machines. In such configurations, robotic collaboration can alleviate the physical demands on workers while maintaining or increasing productivity. Moreover, in contexts like elder care or hospital logistics, cobots offer new ways to support overburdened personnel, handling repetitive or high-effort tasks that would otherwise require constant physical input.

However, these gains are not without countervailing risks. A first area of concern involves psychosocial dynamics in the workplace. As cobots are integrated into workflows, workers may be required to adapt their pace and activity to the rhythm dictated by the machine. This adjustment may result in increased cognitive stress, reduced autonomy, and the perception of surveillance or loss of control. In high-performance industrial settings, this dynamic can exacerbate pressure on operators, especially when output becomes tightly coupled to robotic efficiency.

Second, physical risks persist despite advances in safety design. Collisions between humans and autonomous machines remain possible, particularly in shared workspaces where real-time path prediction and responsive movement are technically complex. While cobots are typically equipped with sensor arrays and programmed to halt upon contact, variations in environment, speed, and human unpredictability introduce a non-negligible margin of error. This is especially critical in high-throughput environments where system latency or miscalibration can result in injury.

Third, the increasing autonomy of robotic systems may paradoxically **reduce the decision-making space** of human workers. In situations where cobots are granted partial authority over sequencing, quality verification, or task prioritization, operators may be relegated to passive monitoring or reactive troubleshooting. This reconfiguration of roles could diminish worker engagement, skill usage, and professional identity, particularly in occupations traditionally rooted in manual expertise or artisanal judgment.

Moreover, the presence of multi-sensorial data collection in robotic systems introduces significant questions about privacy and surveillance. Cobots frequently rely on embedded cameras, motion detectors, thermal sensors, and audio capture to navigate and interpret their environment. In workplaces such as hospitals or care facilities, this raises profound ethical concerns about the intrusiveness of AI-based observation. The deployment of robotic systems in patient rooms, for instance, may violate boundaries of intimacy and compromise the dignity of care recipients, unless governed by strict transparency and data minimization protocols.

From a legal and institutional standpoint, questions of responsibility and liability remain unresolved. In the event of an accident involving a collaborative robot, the allocation of responsibility among manufacturers, integrators, operators, and end users remains legally complex. While most jurisdictions maintain employer responsibility under occupational health frameworks, the emergence of semi-autonomous systems complicates fault attribution, particularly when harm results from interaction errors, software malfunctions, or non-transparent decision-making by the AI subsystem.

For these reasons, the implementation of collaborative robotics must be accompanied by a robust risk governance framework. Organizations must anticipate not only technical risks but also social and psychological effects, ensuring that AI integration reinforces human well-being rather than undermining it. Risk assessments must be participatory, including operators, safety experts, ethicists, and legal counsel, and should guide the design, deployment, and oversight of collaborative systems. Furthermore, transparency about the collection, storage, and use of sensor data is essential to maintain trust and social acceptability in workplaces increasingly shared with machines.

Ultimately, the effective and ethical adoption of collaborative robotics hinges not only on technological maturity, but on a normative commitment to human dignity, autonomy, and safety. As AI technologies advance, the central question will not be whether machines can work alongside humans, but under what conditions, with what safeguards, and to whose benefit.

CHAPTER 5: GOVERNANCE, ETHICS, AND THE STRATEGIC FUTURE OF AI

5.1 The Need for a Human-Centered Governance Framework

The accelerated integration of artificial intelligence (AI) into productive and social structures has revealed a profound asymmetry between the pace of technological innovation and the establishment of regulatory, ethical, and institutional frameworks capable of channeling its impact toward socially desirable outcomes. In this context, the governance of AI must not be reduced to a matter of technical administration or reactive regulation. It must be reconceived as a proactive process of political and normative construction, centered on the preservation and promotion of human dignity, autonomy, and solidarity.

Unlike previous technological revolutions, AI does not only displace or augment human labor; it also affects decision-making processes, value attribution, and responsibility distribution in increasingly opaque systems (Floridi et al., 2018; Russell & Norvig, 2010). This opacity reinforces the need for a governance model that places human beings at the core of algorithmic development and deployment, ensuring that technological systems serve ethical, democratic, and inclusive purposes.

A human-centered governance framework involves three interdependent dimensions. First, the normative dimension refers to the development of ethical and legal principles capable of guiding AI systems from design to implementation. These principles include, but are not limited to, transparency, explainability, justice, accountability, and respect for human rights (Floridi et al., 2018; OECD, 2024). The adoption of these principles should not remain at the declarative level but be accompanied by binding regulations, enforcement mechanisms, and institutional oversight.

Second, the institutional dimension demands the active participation of a plurality of actors—governments, international organizations, companies, labor unions, civil society organizations, and academia—in deliberative processes on the scope, limits, and acceptable uses of AI. Such multi-stakeholder governance not only ensures democratic legitimacy but also facilitates the development of context-sensitive standards. The experience of the European Union's AI Act is a paradigmatic example of regulatory efforts that seek to balance innovation and rights protection.

Third, the operational dimension must ensure that AI systems are designed and deployed in ways that reflect social needs, not just market logic. This includes participatory design processes, impact assessments before and after implementation, and institutional mechanisms for redress in cases of algorithmic harm. Furthermore, it requires investment in public education and digital literacy to equip citizens with the knowledge necessary to understand, critique, and co-determine the role of AI in their lives.

In summary, AI governance must be reconceived not as a technical issue delegated to engineers or market actors, but as a central component of democratic societies in the 21st century. Only by adopting a human-centered framework—normative, institutional, and operational—can we ensure that artificial intelligence contributes to human flourishing rather than undermining the social contract.

5.2 Institutional Design: Regulation, Taxation, and Labor Protection

THE TRANSFORMATIVE power of artificial intelligence (AI) necessitates not only ethical guidelines and governance principles but also concrete institutional mechanisms that can shape, constrain, and direct its development in line with the goals of equity, sustainability, and social justice. In the absence of robust institutions, the deployment of AI tends to follow the path of least resistance: market-driven expansion, asymmetrical data appropriation, and externalization of social costs. This subchapter examines three critical institutional dimensions—regulation, taxation, and labor protection—that must be redefined in the age of AI.

First, regulation must evolve from reactive compliance models to anticipatory governance. Traditional legal frameworks often lag behind technical innovation, creating normative vacuums that can be exploited by private actors (Doshi-Velez & Kim, 2017). To address this, a dynamic regulatory approach is required—one that combines principles-based frameworks with sector-specific standards and is capable of adapting to new risks through continuous monitoring and revision. For instance, real-time algorithmic auditing and risk-tier classification, as established in Regulation (EU) 2024/1689 (the Artificial Intelligence Act), offer a promising direction by calibrating legal obligations according to the potential societal impact of AI applications (OECD, 2024). The Act's implementation record to date, however, illustrates the difficulty with unusual clarity. Its prohibitions on unacceptable-risk practices took effect on 2 February 2025 and its obligations for providers of general-purpose AI models on 2 August 2025, with the general application of the Regulation following on 2 August 2026. The obligations governing high-risk systems—conformity assessment, risk management, data governance, logging, and human oversight, which constitute the substantive core of the framework—were originally scheduled for that same date. They were deferred by the Digital Omnibus on AI, Regulation (EU) 2026/1744, to 2 December 2027 for standalone systems under Annex III and to 2 August 2028 for systems embedded in regulated products under Annex I, pending the publication of harmonised standards.

The sequence is instructive, and it should be read carefully rather than as a simple failure of political will. What entered into force on schedule were the transparency duties under Article 50: obligations to disclose that a user is interacting with a machine and to label synthetic content, with the watermarking requirements of Article 50(2) themselves postponed to 2 December 2026. What was deferred were the provisions that would have required institutions to examine the substance of algorithmic decisions. Disclosure survived contact with implementation; revision did not. This is precisely the asymmetry the present study anticipates. Transparency obligations can be satisfied by describing a system as it operates, an exercise compatible with leaving its operation undisturbed. Substantive review requires an institution to assess whether the regularities a system has encoded should continue to govern, and that capacity proved to be the one the timeline could not sustain. The deferral is not evidence that regulation is impossible; it is evidence that the regulatory instruments developed to date are calibrated for the wrong failure mode, addressing the visibility of automated decisions rather than their revisability. The asymmetry admits a structural explanation, which I have developed at length elsewhere (Startari 2025d). A disclosure obligation is satisfiable by a procedure: it can be specified in advance, discharged by a notice, and verified against a checklist, which is to say it compiles. An obligation to determine whether a system's encoded regularities ought to continue governing cannot be discharged procedurally, because the judgment it requires is precisely the judgment that no rule can specify in advance. Norms that compile are implementable on schedule; norms that require judgment are deferred until the standards arrive, and the standards are themselves attempts to render judgment procedural. On this reading the timeline did not slip for want of political resolve. It slipped because the deferred provisions ask institutions to do the one thing an executable rule cannot do for them. Secondly, taxation must be restructured to address the decoupling between capital and labor in

AI-driven economies. As automation replaces human work in certain sectors, traditional tax systems based on payroll and labor income may become less effective in funding public goods, social security, and training programs (Gans, 2019). Several scholars have proposed mechanisms such as "robot taxes," digital services taxes, or levies on data monetization to ensure that the economic gains from AI are redistributed more fairly (Susskind, 2020). Such reforms are not merely technical, but political: they imply a renegotiation of how value is created and shared in post-industrial economies. Finally, labor protection frameworks must be updated to safeguard workers in the context of increasing algorithmic control and labor fragmentation. The proliferation of gig platforms, algorithmic management systems, and remote microtasking has eroded traditional employment relationships and blurred the boundaries of employer responsibility (Moore, 2019; ILO, 2023). In response, labor institutions must expand their jurisdiction to include non-standard forms of employment, enforce algorithmic transparency in management decisions, and guarantee access to social protections regardless of employment status. This includes not only income support during transitions but also legal empowerment to challenge automated decisions that affect hiring, compensation, or termination. In conclusion, without institutional redesign, the promises of AI—efficiency, scalability, personalization—may coexist with rising inequality, job insecurity, and democratic erosion. It is therefore imperative to implement forward-looking regulatory frameworks, equitable taxation mechanisms, and robust labor protections to ensure that AI serves not only innovation but inclusion. The legitimacy of the AI transition will depend on whether institutions can align technological capabilities with the imperatives of social cohesion and collective well-being.

5.3 The Ethical Imperative: Autonomy, Responsibility, and Transparency

THE ETHICAL GOVERNANCE of artificial intelligence (AI) cannot be conceived as an accessory to innovation; it must be its normative backbone. The increasing integration of AI into critical decision-making processes—ranging from medical diagnostics to judicial risk assessments and employment screening—demands a systematic and enforceable ethical framework that safeguards individual autonomy, clarifies responsibility, and ensures transparency throughout the AI lifecycle (Floridi et al., 2018; Obermeyer et al., 2019).

Autonomy is the cornerstone of liberal democratic societies. Yet, AI systems capable of influencing, recommending, or even deciding on behalf of individuals raise fundamental concerns about the erosion of self-determination. From algorithmic nudges that shape consumer behavior to predictive policing models that anticipate criminal conduct, the subtle power of AI to shape choices challenges traditional conceptions of free will and moral agency (Barocas, Hardt, & Narayanan, 2019). Ethical governance must thus guarantee the right of individuals to opt out of automated systems, access alternative human-based procedures, and be informed of how AI-driven decisions are made.

Responsibility, in the AI context, is diffuse. Traditional models of accountability—where agents are clearly identified and liable for the consequences of their actions—do not easily apply to complex, multi-actor, and sometimes opaque algorithmic systems. Who is responsible when a medical algorithm misdiagnoses a patient? The developer, the data scientist, the institution that deployed the system, or the algorithm itself? To address these ambiguities, a chain-of-responsibility model must be implemented, wherein accountability is distributed but traceable across the AI development and deployment pipeline (Russell & Norvig, 2010). Furthermore, the "right to explanation," already present in the European General Data Protection Regulation (GDPR), must be extended and operationalized in all high-impact AI systems.

Transparency is the precondition for ethical scrutiny and democratic control. However, many AI systems—especially those based on deep learning—operate as "black boxes," making their internal logic inaccessible even to their creators. This epistemic opacity hinders the capacity of users, regulators, and affected individuals to understand, question, or contest automated decisions (Doshi-Velez & Kim, 2017). To address this, explainable AI (XAI) must be prioritized in both research and regulation, ensuring that models used in critical domains can be interpreted, audited, and, if necessary, overruled by human agents.

Moreover, transparency should not be limited to technical aspects but must also extend to data provenance, algorithmic objectives, and value trade-offs. For example, a credit scoring algorithm trained on biased historical data may reproduce social inequalities even if its logic appears statistically sound (Obermeyer et al., 2019). Ethical AI requires not only transparent models but also inclusive design processes where diverse perspectives are incorporated to challenge implicit assumptions and prevent discriminatory outcomes.

In short, autonomy, responsibility, and transparency are not abstract principles but actionable imperatives that must guide every stage of AI development. They are the pillars of a truly human-centered AI: one that not only enhances capabilities but protects dignity, fosters accountability, and reinforces democratic control over increasingly powerful technological systems.

5.4 From Learning Organizations to Societal Learning

THE WIDESPREAD ADOPTION of artificial intelligence (AI) not only redefines work structures and decision-making processes within organizations but also requires a fundamental transformation in how societies generate, distribute, and apply knowledge. While the concept of the "learning organization" has proven effective in promoting adaptability, creativity, and systemic thinking within firms (Senge, 1990), the challenges posed by AI now demand an expansion of this model to encompass society as a whole. This transition toward societal learning is not merely an educational project, but a strategic imperative for democratic resilience and technological co-governance.

Learning organizations—characterized by decentralized decision-making, cross-functional collaboration, and reflexive problem-solving—are particularly well-positioned to foster intelligent human-machine complementarity. They enable continuous upskilling, collective experimentation, and error-based learning that supports both organizational innovation and employee well-being (Kolb, 1984). However, the benefits of this model remain unevenly distributed across sectors and regions, and often limited to high-skill or research-intensive environments. In the age of AI, limiting learning to organizational boundaries is no longer viable.

Societal learning requires that the principles of reflection, systemic feedback, and knowledge democratization be scaled to broader institutional and civic contexts. This involves the integration of lifelong learning policies, participatory innovation ecosystems, and inclusive digital literacy programs. Public institutions, educational systems, media, and civil society must collaborate in cultivating not only technical skills, but also critical thinking, ethical reasoning, and collective foresight. In this way, societal learning becomes the infrastructure through which populations acquire the capacity to navigate, question, and shape algorithmic systems that increasingly permeate all spheres of life (Zawacki-Richter et al., 2019). Moreover, the emergence of algorithmic governance—where decisions once made by humans are now partially or fully delegated to machines—requires that citizens themselves become epistemically empowered. That is, they must understand how data are collected, how models are trained, and what values are embedded in AI systems. This epistemic empowerment is not equivalent to technical expertise, but rather to the development of cognitive and democratic capacities that enable meaningful participation in decisions about technology. Without such societal literacy, the asymmetry between technological elites and the general population will widen, leading to a deficit of democratic legitimacy and public trust. In parallel, policy frameworks must evolve to recognize and support informal, community-based, and experiential learning as valid and essential. Learning does not happen exclusively within schools or corporations; it emerges in social networks, peer groups, and activist communities engaging with the consequences of AI in real time. Institutional recognition of these practices—as well as support for citizen science, participatory technology assessment, and bottom-up innovation—can greatly enrich the societal capacity to learn and adapt in the face of rapid technological change. In conclusion, fostering intelligent complementarity between humans and AI cannot be achieved through technical interventions alone. It requires a societal infrastructure of learning—reflexive, participatory, and distributed—that empowers individuals and communities to co-shape the evolution of technology. From this broader perspective, learning is not simply a tool of economic adaptation, but a means of cultivating social autonomy, ethical deliberation, and collective agency in the AI era.

5.5 Long-Term Strategies: Innovation, Equity, and Resilience

ARTIFICIAL INTELLIGENCE (AI) is not a passing technological wave—it constitutes a structural transformation whose long-term implications extend beyond productivity gains or economic disruption. The way societies respond to AI today will determine not only the configuration of labor markets and industrial ecosystems, but also the ethical foundations, institutional capacities, and social cohesion of future generations. In this context, long-term strategies must be framed around three fundamental axes: innovation, equity, and resilience.

First, innovation policy must shift from a purely competitive logic to one that is also mission-oriented and socially embedded. AI development should not be confined to private research agendas or efficiency-maximizing applications. Instead, it should be steered toward solving grand societal challenges: climate change, public health, educational equity, and democratic participation (Mazzucato, 2018). Public investment and regulation should thus promote "purpose-driven innovation," where AI contributes to inclusive and sustainable development rather than reinforcing existing asymmetries of power and access.

Second, equity must be placed at the center of AI governance. This involves designing technological infrastructures that are accessible, interoperable, and inclusive by default. In practice, this means combating algorithmic discrimination, ensuring equitable access to high-quality training programs, and building redistributive mechanisms (e.g., digital dividends, universal data income, public AI platforms) that democratize the benefits of AI across populations and geographies (Susskind, 2020). Without a deliberate effort to address inequality, AI may exacerbate structural disadvantages, both within and between countries.

Third, resilience must be redefined not merely as the capacity to "bounce back" after disruption, but as the systemic ability to anticipate, absorb, and adapt to complex change. In a world increasingly shaped by interdependent crises—pandemics, geopolitical instability, supply chain fragility, environmental degradation—AI can play a vital role in supporting anticipatory governance. This includes early-warning systems, crisis simulation models, dynamic resource allocation, and real-time risk assessment. However, resilience also demands the preservation of human judgment, ethical deliberation, and institutional learning mechanisms that can mediate between technological possibilities and social values (OECD, 2024).

Strategically, fostering innovation, equity, and resilience requires coordination across levels of governance: international agreements on AI standards and ethics; national policies on education, taxation, and labor; and local initiatives that contextualize AI deployment according to specific community needs. Long-term strategies also require temporal awareness. Policy frameworks must include forward-looking indicators, scenario modeling, and foresight exercises to explore alternative futures, avoid path dependencies, and correct courses where necessary (UNESCO, 2021). In sum, AI policy cannot remain reactive, fragmented, or technocratic. It must be reimagined as a multidimensional architecture that aligns technological progress with collective purpose, distributes its benefits fairly, and fortifies society against the shocks and uncertainties of the 21st century. This is not simply a matter of managing innovation but of governing the future.

5.6 Research Gaps and Multistakeholder Dialogue

DESPITE THE GROWING body of literature on the economic, social, and ethical implications of artificial intelligence (AI), significant research gaps remain. These gaps not only hinder our ability to understand the full impact of AI on work and society but also limit the effectiveness of public policies and institutional responses. Bridging these gaps requires a concerted effort to integrate multidisciplinary research approaches with inclusive, participatory dialogue involving a wide range of stakeholders.

One of the primary limitations in existing research is the scarcity of high-quality, disaggregated data on AI adoption at the organizational level. Most quantitative studies rely on macroeconomic indicators or generalized estimates of "automation potential," often based on task-based taxonomies rather than real-world implementations (Holm & Lorenz, 2022). As a result, the nuances of how AI is actually integrated into production processes, labor relations, and decision-making frameworks remain largely understudied. Furthermore, little is known about the internal dynamics of firms—strategic choices, cost structures, organizational resistance, and management practices—that shape the success or failure of AI deployment.

There is also a lack of robust methodologies for evaluating the long-term and systemic effects of AI. While algorithmic impact assessments have been proposed in some jurisdictions, they remain underdeveloped and rarely applied in practice (Doshi-Velez & Kim, 2017). Sector-specific studies, particularly in low- and middle-income countries, are severely underrepresented, creating a biased understanding of global trends and masking the differentiated impacts across geographies, industries, and socio-professional categories. To overcome these challenges, new empirical instruments must be designed—surveys tailored to the realities of workers, companies, and institutional actors, capable of capturing the complexity of algorithmic transformations in context. Case study protocols and semi-structured interviews with diverse stakeholders—AI users, developers, regulators, labor representatives—can enrich our understanding of how ethical principles are translated (or not) into practice. Such qualitative approaches are essential for exploring key questions: How do organizations define "responsible AI"? What are the main barriers to implementing explainability, fairness, or redress mechanisms? What forms of worker involvement exist in AI-related decisions? In parallel, the design of human–machine interfaces and their cognitive and ergonomic impacts remain underexplored. Research must investigate how these interfaces influence attention, judgment, autonomy, and responsibility, and how they reshape the relationship between expertise and machine-generated output (Voss, 2021). A better understanding of these dynamics is essential for ensuring that AI systems enhance rather than undermine human capabilities. Multistakeholder dialogue is not simply a mechanism of consultation—it is an epistemic necessity. The legitimacy and effectiveness of AI governance depend on including those most affected by the technology. Governments, unions, civil society organizations, academia, industry, and end users must participate in the co-design of AI systems and in setting the boundaries of their use. Participatory mechanisms such as citizens' assemblies, ethical review boards, and workplace-level algorithmic councils can help institutionalize this dialogue. In conclusion, closing the research and governance gaps surrounding AI requires a double movement: expanding our empirical and theoretical tools, and broadening the democratic base of technological decision-making. Only through inclusive, context-sensitive, and interdisciplinary inquiry can we build the institutional intelligence necessary to navigate an AI-driven future with foresight and justice.

CHAPTER 6: THE CLOSURE OF INSTITUTIONAL FUTURES

6.1 Restating the Argument Against the Evidence

The five preceding chapters were written, in their earlier editions, as a survey. They remain a survey, and nothing in them has been withdrawn. But they were also, without my having recognized it at the time, an accumulation of evidence for a single proposition, and this chapter states the proposition against the evidence assembled rather than in advance of it.

The proposition is that artificial intelligence, as presently constituted, is an instrument of conservation rather than transformation, and that its principal danger lies not in what it displaces but in what it renders difficult to reconsider.

Chapter 1 established why this follows from the structure of the technology rather than from any particular application of it. A system that derives its parameters from recorded observation can project only the regularities that observation contains. Neither scale nor extended inference alters this; the first enlarges the deposit of precedent and the second searches it more thoroughly. The faculty that inductive systems lack is not computational power or persistence but the capacity to recognize a regularity as unjust and to refuse it on that ground, which is the faculty by which institutions revise themselves.

Chapter 2 supplied an unexpected corroboration. The evaluation frameworks developed to assess these systems—accuracy, precision, recall, and the fairness metrics layered above them—all measure fidelity to a benchmark, and every benchmark is a record of the past. A system that reproduced historical arrangements with perfect fidelity would score well on every metric in current use. The instruments built to detect algorithmic harm are therefore constitutionally unable to detect the conservation effect, because conservation registers on them as success. This is worth stating plainly: the field's evaluative apparatus is not merely silent on the problem identified here but actively obscures it.

Chapter 3 explained a failure that has puzzled the labor economics literature for a decade. Employment projections have been consistently unreliable—Frey and Osborne's forty-seven percent, the substantially lower task-based estimates that followed, the persistent gap between predicted and observed displacement. The standard diagnosis attributes this to methodological immaturity. The diagnosis offered here is different: the projections fail because they extrapolate occupational categories while the technology is simultaneously freezing those categories in place. A forecast that treats its own unit of analysis as stable, when the deployment under study is what stabilizes it, cannot succeed. The methodology is not too crude. It is measuring a variable the phenomenon has made endogenous.

Chapter 4 furnished the mechanism in three sectors. Healthcare, transportation, and banking differ in every relevant respect—regulatory density, capital intensity, tolerance for error, the degree to which their core work is codifiable. In all three, the pace and shape of adoption were determined not by technical capability but by relative costs, and in all three those relative costs proved to be artifacts of institutional arrangement rather than facts of engineering. Labor remains cheaper than automation in textiles, in recycling, in food preparation, and it remains cheaper because of what is taxed, what is protected, what is subsidized, and what liability attaches to whom. The technology did not set these terms. It inherited them, encoded them, and now propagates them at a speed at which they are no longer examined.

Chapter 5 recorded what happened when an institution attempted to intervene. The European Union's Artificial Intelligence Act is the most ambitious regulatory instrument yet directed at these systems, and its implementation divided along a line the present argument predicts. The obligations that could be discharged procedurally—disclosure, labelling, notification—entered into force on schedule. The obligations that required an institution to determine whether a system's encoded regularities ought to continue governing were deferred by more than a year, pending standards that are themselves attempts to render that determination procedural. Disclosure compiles. Judgment does not.

6.2 What Follows for Governance

IF THE DIAGNOSIS IS correct, a substantial part of the governance apparatus assembled over the past decade is addressed to the wrong problem. This is not an argument against regulation, and it should not be mistaken for one. It is an argument that the instruments currently favored are calibrated for disruption when the failure mode is fixation.

The distinction has practical content. Consider what follows from each diagnosis. If artificial intelligence is disruptive, the appropriate instruments are those that slow deployment and contain harm: moratoria, risk tiers, conformity assessment, impact statements filed before systems enter service. Each of these is a brake, and a brake is the correct response to something moving too fast in a fixed direction. If artificial intelligence is conservative in the sense argued here, brakes are close to useless and may be worse than useless, because the danger is not velocity but the progressive elimination of the capacity to steer. A system that has slowed the encoding of historical arrangements has not thereby acquired the ability to revise them.

What the diagnosis recommends instead is institutional capacity of a different kind, and I state four requirements without supposing the list complete.

The first is mandatory periodic reconsideration, distinguished sharply from periodic audit. An audit asks whether a system performs as specified. Reconsideration asks whether the specification should stand—whether the categories a system operates upon, the thresholds it applies, and the outcomes it treats as success remain defensible on grounds independent of the fact that they were previously adopted. This cannot be discharged by measurement, because it is precisely the question measurement presupposes an answer to. It requires a body with the authority to conclude that a functioning system should be altered or withdrawn, and a schedule on which that body is obliged to reach a conclusion.

There is now direct evidence that the mechanism this book describes is measurable, and I set it out here because a thesis that generates a measurable prediction is in a different position from one that does not.

In a controlled study of instruction templates (Startari 2025f), I examined how the fixed textual scaffolding that governs model behavior in institutional settings redistributes decision rights in the resulting outputs. The design used a synthetic corpus of one thousand prompts drawn from five institutional domains, each executed under five template conditions, yielding five thousand generated texts. Seven indicators were operationalized to capture where authority resides in a text rather than whether the text is accurate: the ratio of delegated to retained decisions, the number of available veto paths, the strength of default scope, the rate of agent deletion, the depth of deontic stacking, the presence of escalation clauses, and the friction attached to overriding a recommendation. Estimation used mixed-effects models with intra-prompt comparison; twenty percent of the corpus was double-coded blind to assess inter-annotator agreement; template ablations, adversarial prompts, and placebo reformulations were used to separate authority effects from stylistic variation; and familywise error was controlled across the seven indicators.

The finding is that minor variations in instruction templates produce systematic and measurable reallocations of authority in institutional text. A template that phrases a recommendation as a default rather than an option, or omits an escalation route, or deletes the agent from a consequential clause, shifts the locus of decision without altering the substantive content of the output and without any participant deciding that the shift should occur.

The relevance to the present argument is direct, and also limited in a way worth stating. The study establishes that the arrangements a system encodes can be detected and quantified at the level of text, and that they change under interventions no one would classify as substantive. This is the conservation mechanism operating at the smallest observable scale, and it is where the thesis first becomes falsifiable in practice: had template variation produced no systematic reallocation, the claim that these systems fix institutional arrangements through ordinary operation would have lost an important part of its support. What the study does not establish is the further proposition that such reallocations persist and compound over institutional time, which is the claim Chapter 6 advances and which would require longitudinal observation of deployed systems rather than a controlled corpus. The measurement demonstrates the mechanism; the historical claim remains an inference from it.

This is not to say that no further measurement is possible, and the qualification matters because a requirement that admits of no instrumentation tends to go unimplemented. What conventional metrics cannot detect, as argued above, is conservation itself, since fidelity to a historical benchmark registers on them as success. But indicators can be constructed that measure something else. In work on AI-mediated conflict discourse (Startari 2026c) I have proposed an agency-preservation rate, which measures not whether a party is represented but whether it retains the grammatical position of an agent—examining subject position, verbal agency, passive attribution, agent deletion, and the conversion of actors into risk objects. The construction generalizes beyond that domain. An indicator of this type does not ask whether a system is accurate; it asks what the system's output does to the standing of those it describes, which is a question about conserved arrangement rather than about correspondence to a benchmark. A complementary approach operates at the level of the clause rather than the actor. In work on the governance of foundation models (Startari 2025g) I have proposed decomposing generated institutional text into a finite set of clause types—commitments, authorizations, restrictions, prescriptions, exemptions, deferrals—each corresponding to a distinct governance act, and measuring the resulting distribution: what proportion of required clause types a system actually produces, and whether prohibited types appear in contexts where they are disallowed. The advantage of this construction for the argument developed here is that it requires no access to model weights or training data. It operates on the surface structure of the output, which means it can be applied by a regulator, an auditor, or an affected institution rather than only by the party that built the system — a consideration that matters given that the entity best positioned to detect conservation is rarely the entity with an interest in detecting it.

Instruments of this kind are what periodic reconsideration would require in order to become an auditable obligation rather than an aspiration. The tractable research task the present argument implies is less their invention, which is largely done, than their institutionalization.

The second is the preservation of institutional memory of alternatives. Once a predictive system is integrated into a decision process, the arrangements it displaced cease to be practiced, and within a generation of professional turnover they cease to be known. The capacity to revise depends on the availability of something to revise toward; an institution that has forgotten how a decision was made before automation cannot evaluate the automation against anything but itself. This is an archival and pedagogical obligation, and it is unglamorous, and it is nonetheless load-bearing.

The third is the protection of the authority to overrule, understood as a structural rather than a formal guarantee. Most deployments nominally preserve human override. In practice the override is exercised rarely and at professional cost: it requires the individual to accept personal liability for departing from a determination the institution has validated, and the incentive gradient runs uniformly toward deference. A right to overrule that is costly to exercise is not a safeguard but a formality. Making it real requires that departure from algorithmic recommendation be treated as an ordinary exercise of professional judgment rather than as an exception demanding justification—which is to say, it requires reversing the presumption that current practice has installed.

The fourth follows from Chapter 4 and is the most demanding. If relative costs are institutional artifacts, they are legitimate objects of deliberate policy rather than parameters to be accepted. The question of whether labor or capital is cheaper in a given sector is not answered by the state of the art; it is answered by taxation, liability allocation, social protection, and the terms of employment law. Treating these as fixed while treating automation as inevitable inverts the actual order of determination. The arrangements are the variable. The technology adapts to them.

6.3 The Limits of the Argument

AN ARGUMENT THAT CANNOT state what would defeat it is not an argument. I therefore set out what would defeat this one.

The thesis fails if generative systems are shown to originate categories genuinely absent from their training distributions—not novel recombinations of learned elements, which are abundant and not at issue, but conceptual structures that cannot be reconstructed as recombination. I do not believe current evidence establishes this, and I have set out in Chapter 1 why extended inference does not supply it. But the question is empirical and the evidence is accumulating, and a demonstration of the requisite kind would require the abandonment of the central claim rather than its qualification.

The thesis is now also testable in a narrower and more immediate sense, which is a recent development and an improvement in its standing. If the indicators described in the preceding section were applied across template variants, model families, and institutional domains and returned no systematic reallocation of authority—if the locus of decision in generated text proved invariant to the scaffolding that produces it—then the claim that these systems fix arrangements through ordinary operation would be substantially undermined at its foundation. The controlled evidence available indicates otherwise, but it is one study on a synthetic corpus, and the appropriate response to a single study is replication rather than confidence. The instruments and the annotated corpus have been released for that purpose.

The thesis is substantially weakened if institutions prove more capable of periodic reconsideration than the record so far suggests. The argument's force depends on an asymmetry between the speed of encoding and the speed of revision. Should the deferred provisions of the Artificial Intelligence Act enter into force in 2027 and 2028 and prove effective in practice—should institutions demonstrate that they can and will overturn functioning systems on normative grounds—then the closure I describe is a transitional difficulty rather than a structural condition, and the appropriate response is patience rather than redesign. I would welcome this outcome and do not expect it.

The thesis is narrower than adjacent arguments with which it might be conflated, and I want to distinguish it from them. It is not a claim that these systems are ineffective; they are frequently effective, and the argument concerns what their effectiveness consists in. It is not a claim that automation reduces employment; that question is addressed in Chapter 3 and the answer given there is that the evidence is mixed and the forecasts unreliable. It is not a claim that human cognition is exempt from computational description, a metaphysical position on which nothing here depends. And it is not a claim that algorithmic bias is the central problem, though bias is one visible symptom of the conservation the thesis identifies. The argument is narrower than any of these: that inductive systems can only conserve, that they conserve faster than institutions revise, and that the resulting closure has been largely absent from a literature preoccupied with disruption.

6.4 The Question Restated

THE SECOND EDITION of this book asked how we might ensure that artificial intelligence serves the human rather than reshaping the human to serve the machine. The question was too generous to itself, in a way I did not see at the time. It assumed a stable subject—a "we" with settled purposes—that might direct the technology toward its ends. But the capacity to have purposes that depart from inherited arrangement is precisely the capacity the deployment described here erodes. A society that has delegated its consequential judgments to systems structurally incapable of departing from precedent will not experience this as coercion. It will experience it as the absence of any alternative worth considering, which is a far more durable condition than coercion and requires no one to enforce it.

The question that replaces it is narrower and harder to evade. Not what artificial intelligence will do to work, nor how many jobs will remain, nor whether the systems can be made transparent. The question is whether the institutions now deploying these technologies will retain the capacity to conclude that some part of what they have inherited ought to be otherwise—and to act on that conclusion against the weight of a system that has already determined the matter, correctly, on the evidence of the past.

That capacity is not a technical property. No architecture supplies it and no metric detects its absence. It is a property of institutions, sustained by deliberate design or lost by default, and on the present evidence it is being lost by default. Whether that continues is not a prediction the argument of this book is competent to make. It is a decision, which is the point.

CONCLUSION: ARTIFICIAL INTELLIGENCE AND THE FUTURE OF HUMAN-CENTERED WORK

In recent years, artificial intelligence has become the object of intense scientific, political, and public debate, primarily due to its far-reaching economic and social implications. The central axis of these debates revolves around questions that remain both fundamental and unresolved: to what extent can machines replace human labor? How many jobs will be created and destroyed? How will occupations, skills, and working conditions be transformed through the deployment of artificial intelligence across sectors?

Available forecasts—whether optimistic or alarmist—have thus far failed to provide reliable answers to these legitimate concerns. On one hand, excessive optimism tends to generate unrealistic expectations about the technical capacities of AI, its contribution to productivity growth, and its assumed potential to improve working conditions or foster harmonious collaboration between humans and machines. On the other hand, the most pessimistic estimations promote a discourse of inevitable disruption, often projecting scenarios of massive job destruction, erosion of worker autonomy, and the progressive dehumanization of labor.

Both discourses suffer from reductionism and offer limited heuristic value. Overly optimistic perspectives risk obscuring the institutional and material conditions necessary for AI to remain a tool in the service of human flourishing. Conversely, excessive pessimism may lead to a defensive posture, causing society to renounce the benefits of technological innovation and adopt a passive stance that neglects the urgent task of preparing workers and institutions for forthcoming changes. These two extremes ultimately inhibit the formulation of proactive, inclusive, and well-governed pathways for AI integration.

In this context, it is essential to promote a realistic and pragmatic approach that enables the development of artificial intelligence to be framed as a means for enhancing individual and collective well-being. The sectoral case studies presented in this volume demonstrate that AI introduces both risks—such as the delegation of knowledge to opaque systems and the deterioration of working conditions in the name of efficiency—and opportunities, including the enrichment of tasks, the elevation of human skills, and the potential empowerment of workers through new organizational paradigms.

What emerges, therefore, is a paradoxical landscape, where risk and value coexist. The central conclusion is that the effects of artificial intelligence on employment and work are not determined by the technology itself, but by the frameworks established by human societies for its design, deployment, and regulation. The history of technological change confirms that its consequences are not automatic or linear, but contingent on institutional decisions, cultural norms, power dynamics, and governance structures.

The question is not whether AI will transform work—this transformation is already underway—but how, under what terms, and toward which ends. The challenge is thus less technological than profoundly anthropological, ethical, and political. We must ask ourselves what kind of work and society we aspire to build, and what role we wish to reserve for human intelligence, empathy, and judgment. Artificial intelligence compels us to reflect on these foundational issues, and its evolution will be shaped by the answers we give to such questions.

This also entails articulating a vision of complementarity between AI and human capacities, rather than a vision of replacement. While AI systems may be unpredictable and capable of disruptive innovation, their integration into society must be evaluated not only through technical parameters but within a normative and ethical framework. Such a framework already exists at the macro-political level and is enshrined in documents like the United Nations Charter and the Universal Declaration of Human Rights, which may serve as foundations for orienting technological development in ways that respect human dignity, autonomy, and equality.

Ultimately, the trajectory that artificial intelligence will follow is not an inevitability. It is the result of collective choices. Technologists, analysts, and workers will operate within the parameters society chooses to define. Their experiences can either be shaped by precarization and algorithmic subordination, or by dignified, meaningful, and stable labor relations—depending on the direction set by public policy, institutional design, and civic values.

The possibility that artificial intelligence may eventually replace a vast portion of human labor is no longer confined to speculative fiction. The progress achieved in recent years demonstrates that AI is capable not only of executing routine and repetitive operations with unmatched speed and precision, but also of performing tasks traditionally associated with high cognitive value and professional expertise. Domains once thought to be insulated from automation—such as medicine, law, engineering, and even artistic creation—are now directly impacted by systems capable of diagnosing illnesses, drafting contracts, designing infrastructure, composing music, and generating images. This evolution raises a series of unprecedented social, economic, and ethical dilemmas.

In such a scenario, excessive dependence on AI could generate structural inequality. The ownership of data, computational infrastructure, and algorithmic design is increasingly concentrated in a small number of global actors—mostly large multinational corporations and technologically advanced states. These actors possess the capacity to design, train, and commercialize AI systems, positioning themselves as gatekeepers of access to employment, information, and social services. Meanwhile, vast segments of the population risk being displaced or excluded from productive activity, further exacerbating the divide between those who control technology and those who are subjected to it.

The danger is not limited to material deprivation. A society in which decision-making is increasingly delegated to opaque algorithms may also experience a progressive erosion of civic autonomy and critical judgment. As individuals become accustomed to relying on intelligent systems for decisions in consumption, mobility, communication, or even politics, there is a risk of outsourcing responsibility and weakening public deliberation. This loss of agency could foster passivity, discourage engagement, and ultimately erode the foundations of democratic life. The problem is not merely technical but ontological: the risk is that we cease to act as autonomous subjects, becoming mere users or spectators in a system driven by machinic logic.

In the long term, the massive replacement of human work by AI could trigger a profound existential crisis. Work has historically been a central dimension of human identity, social belonging, and personal purpose. If AI renders human labor obsolete, it may disrupt the very conditions that give meaning and structure to individual lives and communities. The resulting alienation could lead to psychological distress, loss of self-esteem, and a generalized sense of uselessness, particularly in populations for whom work represents the primary vector of social integration.

The hypothetical case of a low-income family whose economic survival depends on the mother's work as a taxi or truck driver illustrates the concrete consequences of such displacement. The automation of driving eliminates her occupation, drastically reducing the family's income and ability to meet basic needs. Educational opportunities for her children diminish, social mobility becomes inaccessible, and a spiral of poverty deepens. Beyond material deprivation, the mother's identity and sense of dignity are directly affected. In a labor market dominated by AI, where alternative employment paths are scarce or nonexistent, reintegration becomes an increasingly implausible prospect. The family as a whole is plunged into social vulnerability, and the disjunction between winners and losers in the AI transition becomes a breeding ground for frustration, conflict, and instability.

The emergence and expansion of artificial intelligence across labor systems introduce not only economic and functional disruptions, but also deep transformations in the meaning, experience, and control of work. In certain sectors, AI reinforces highly fragmented and repetitive tasks, reviving the risk of alienation that had been partially mitigated by previous labor reforms. This is particularly visible in logistics and warehouse environments, where automation has reorganized tasks into mechanized sequences, reducing workers to functional appendices within algorithmically controlled systems.

Case studies in large distribution centers demonstrate how AI-guided processes, such as automated sorting and robotic palletization, have narrowed human activity into a set of predefined gestures. In these contexts, workers report sensations of depersonalization and loss of agency, as they are no longer autonomous operators but reactive agents subordinated to machine-directed flows. This phenomenon has been exacerbated by digital platforms such as Amazon Mechanical Turk, where human labor is modularized into microtasks and managed remotely via algorithmic coordination. Here, the resemblance to the Taylorist model of fragmented labor is stark, though intensified by the virtual and real-time dimension of control. Moreover, the integration of AI into the workplace increases the potential for surveillance and data-driven disciplinary regimes. While surveillance in labor is not a novel phenomenon, the volume, granularity, and behavioral scope of data collected by AI systems far exceed previous modalities. Even so-called collaborative robots, designed to assist workers, generate vast amounts of information about workflow rhythms, productivity, rest intervals, interpersonal interactions, and even inferred emotional states. Depending on the organizational culture and managerial philosophy, these data streams may be used to optimize productivity or to amplify monitoring and performance pressure. Such practices can foster stress, anxiety, and psychosocial fatigue, contributing to a work environment marked by mistrust and instrumentalization.

This dynamic recalls earlier debates about technological deskilling—the deliberate fragmentation of tasks to reduce worker autonomy and enhance managerial control. The introduction of numerically controlled machines in the 20th century, which separated design from execution, was one example of such a strategy. Today, artificial intelligence reactivates this concern on a broader scale, posing risks not only to manual workers but also to highly qualified professionals. In a context where algorithms perform increasingly complex tasks, human expertise risks being marginalized, leading to disengagement, resistance to innovation, and a breakdown in cooperative practices. At the heart of this issue lies a more fundamental challenge: the epistemological asymmetry between algorithmic systems and human users. AI models operate through the extraction of statistical patterns from historical data, a process which tends to replicate past regularities and inhibit creative rupture. Innovation, by contrast, requires the capacity to break rules, to imagine alternative futures, and to challenge inherited assumptions. Humans must therefore retain the critical responsibility of contextualizing, questioning, and sometimes rejecting AI recommendations. This demands that algorithmic systems be transparent and auditable, allowing users to trace the logic, parameters, and data sets underpinning machine decisions.

The excessive transfer of decision-making to machines may erode this responsibility. When workers begin to assume that algorithms are infallible or non-negotiable, the result is a loss of accountability and interpretative initiative. The erosion is not merely a matter of disposition, of workers becoming credulous or incurious in the presence of authoritative-seeming output. There is a structural dimension to it: a system that produces a determination without producing the grounds on which that determination might be contested leaves nothing for interpretative initiative to act upon, and the trace that would permit ethical evaluation is not concealed but absent (Startari 2025e). Deference, under such conditions, is less a failure of professional character than the only available response to an output that cannot be argued with. This matters for remedy. If the problem were disposition, training in critical scrutiny would address it. If the problem is that the object of scrutiny has no contestable structure, the remedy must be sought in how systems are built and how the institutions using them allocate the authority to overrule. This trend is particularly acute among highly skilled professionals, who may feel displaced or disempowered by algorithmic systems that appear to operate with superior speed, scope, and accuracy. Organizational cultures that reinforce such asymmetry risk fostering opposition, organizational fatigue, and a collapse in professional morale. To address these challenges, institutions must prioritize the development of hybrid decision-support systems in which AI expertise is integrated with the domain-specific knowledge of workers. Co-design, participatory modeling, and interface tailoring are essential for ensuring that AI tools are aligned with the needs, constraints, and judgment frameworks of their users. Such integration not only enhances the validity of outputs, but also promotes user acceptance, reduces systemic risks, and reinforces the legitimacy of AI deployment in sensitive environments.

This imperative extends to the educational and training systems, both at the initial and continuing levels. Learning to interact with intelligent systems requires more than technical proficiency. It demands the cultivation of critical thinking, systemic reasoning, creativity, reflexivity, and collective problem-solving skills. Individuals must be equipped to discern interdependent phenomena, to evaluate the limits of algorithmic reasoning, and to formulate operational solutions that are ethically sound and socially responsive. In this sense, training for the age of AI must go beyond tool usage to foster a new humanism of competence, where knowledge, ethics, and autonomy converge.

The profound transformations driven by artificial intelligence call for a redefinition of education and training systems on an unprecedented scale. In contrast to previous industrial revolutions—where technological adaptation followed relatively linear learning curves—AI evolves through recursive feedback, rendering obsolete not only specific skills but entire professional paradigms. As AI assumes an increasing number of cognitive and operational tasks, the longevity of skills shortens, and the imperative for continuous learning becomes universal.

In this context, reskilling and upskilling strategies are not merely economic imperatives; they are ethical and political commitments to inclusion, agency, and human dignity. Support for workers exposed to automation must involve clear career pathways, mobility mechanisms across sectors, and training programs that are consistent with the dynamic evolution of knowledge. These programs must transcend formal instruction and encompass experiential learning—emphasizing trial and error, problem-solving, creativity, and risk management. The objective is not only to transfer technical proficiency, but to cultivate the capacity to learn how to learn, while reinforcing individual responsibility and ethical discernment in decision-making.

Yet public policy alone is insufficient. The internal dynamics of organizations—their management culture, task structure, and learning modalities—are equally decisive in shaping how AI transforms work. Among existing organizational models, the learning organization stands out as the most promising framework for fostering intelligent complementarity between humans and machines. Defined by its capacity to continuously adapt through shared learning processes, the learning organization promotes autonomy, interdisciplinary collaboration, and systemic thinking. Within such organizations, mistakes are not penalized but reframed as opportunities for innovation, reflection, and cognitive growth. By fostering interdisciplinary knowledge exchange, the learning organization equips its members not only to perform their tasks but to understand how those tasks relate to broader systemic challenges. This holistic perspective enhances problem-solving, critical judgment, and adaptive capacity—all attributes that AI systems, despite their computational power, cannot replicate. From this standpoint, the workplace becomes a locus not of routinization but of collective intelligence. It is within such configurations that the ethical and strategic governance of AI can be most effectively realized.

This transformation, however, must be supported by macro-level institutional frameworks. Governments and international organizations must not only fund training programs, but also facilitate organizational change and workplace learning as critical pillars of the AI transition. This becomes especially urgent in the face of concurrent global challenges—geopolitical instability, economic stagnation, and climate crises—that intersect with and amplify the disruptive effects of digital automation. The organizations of tomorrow must be resilient not only in the face of technological change, but of structural complexity itself.

Prospective studies suggest that the ability to manage complexity will be a decisive factor in organizational survival and innovation by 2030. However, whether AI will mitigate or exacerbate this complexity remains uncertain. What is clear is that societies must equip themselves not only to absorb change, but to steer it toward collectively defined goals. Strengthening applied research into the real effects of AI on work is therefore a top priority. Current methodologies remain inadequate, and microdata-based analyses—while promising—are limited by availability and scope. Future surveys must be enriched with data on internal organizational dynamics, implementation costs, decision-making processes, and the lived experiences of employees. Only with this level of granularity can we assess whether AI deployment respects ethical principles and contributes to sustainable development.

Case studies at the sectoral level must be integrated into this research agenda. These studies can explore key issues: the extent to which transparency is operationalized in AI systems; how workers' data is collected, labeled, and used; whether algorithmic outputs are questioned and refined by human users; and how interfaces between humans and algorithms affect cognitive and emotional capacities. Such inquiries must also account for sectoral variations, socio-professional inequalities, and the differing impacts of AI depending on occupational status and task configuration.

Underlying all of these reflections is a fundamental political economy question: the relationship between capital costs and labor costs. The mere existence of a technological solution does not ensure its adoption. In many sectors—such as textiles, recycling, or fast-food preparation—labor remains cheaper than automation. The relative cost of capital versus labor is shaped not by technology, but by institutions, regulation, taxation, and social protection systems. These mechanisms define the contours of AI deployment. They determine whether AI becomes a force for equity and cohesion or an accelerator of inequality and precarity.

Therefore, the core issue is not how many jobs AI might eliminate, but rather what kind of society we wish to build. Our relationship with technology will be a mirror of our collective values and our normative commitments. The future of work will not be determined by algorithms, but by the frameworks we choose to establish—ethical, institutional, and civic—through which innovation can be directed toward human flourishing, democratic renewal, and shared prosperity.

BIBLIOGRAPHY

A note on the author's own works cited. This volume draws at several points on a parallel line of research conducted by the author under the series titles Grammars of Power, Executable Legitimacy, and AI Syntactic Power and Legitimacy. Those works approach the questions treated here through the analysis of syntax, attribution, and legitimacy rather than through epistemology, and they are cited where their conclusions bear on the present argument or where they develop a mechanism at greater length than is possible in this volume. Several are deposited in open archives (Zenodo, Figshare) with assigned DOIs but have not yet received SSRN identifiers or completed peer review; this is indicated in each entry. The reader should weigh them accordingly. They are cited as convergent lines of inquiry, not as external corroboration, and the argument of this book does not depend on any of them: the epistemological claim advanced in Chapter 1 stands or falls on its own terms and on the independent empirical and regulatory evidence assembled in Chapters 3 through 5.

Acemoglu, D., & Restrepo, P. (2020). Robots and jobs: Evidence from US labor markets. Journal of Political Economy, 128(6), 2188-2244.

Agrawal, A., Gans, J., & Goldfarb, A. (2019). The Economics of Artificial Intelligence: An Agenda. University of Chicago Press.

Autor, D., & Handel, M. (2013). Putting tasks to the test: Human capital, job tasks, and wages. Journal of Labor Economics, 31(S1), S59–S96.

Autor, D., Mindell, D., & Reynolds, E. (2021). The Work of the Future: Building Better Jobs in an Age of Intelligent Machines. MIT Task Force on the Work of the Future.

Angwin, J., Larson, J., Mattu, S., & Kirchner, L. (2016). Machine bias: There's software used across the country to predict future criminals. And it's biased against blacks. ProPublica, May 23, 2016.

Barocas, S., Hardt, M., & Narayanan, A. (2019). Fairness and Machine Learning. fairmlbook.org.

Benhamou, F. (2018). La déqualification par les technologies numériques. In F. Vatin, L. Merzeau, & J. Bonaccorsi (Eds.), Travail et Numérique: Questions de sociologie (pp. 21-33). Presses des Mines.

Benhamou, S., & Lorenz, E. (2020). Organizational issues in training and job quality. Trabajo y Sociedad, (34), 313-334.

Arntz, M., Gregory, T., & Zierahn, U. (2016). The Risk of Automation for Jobs in OECD Countries: A Comparative Analysis. OECD Social, Employment and Migration Working Papers, No. 189. Paris: OECD Publishing.

Besold, T. R., d'Avila Garcez, A., Bader, S., Bowman, H., Domingos, P., Hitzler, P., et al. (2017). Neural-symbolic learning and reasoning: A survey and interpretation. arXiv:1711.03902.

Bessen, J. (2019). AI and Jobs: The Role of Demand. NBER Working Paper No. 24235. Cambridge, MA: National Bureau of Economic Research.

Boddington, P. (2017). Towards a Code of Ethics for Artificial Intelligence. Cham: Springer.

Bohbot, V. D., Lerch, J., Thorndycraft, B., Iaria, G., & Zijdenbos, A. P. (2017). Gray matter differences correlate with spontaneous strategies in a human virtual navigation task. The Journal of Neuroscience, 37(13), 3470-3484.

Brundage, M., Avin, S., Wang, J., Belfield, H., Krueger, G., Hadfield, G., et al. (2020). Toward trustworthy AI development: Mechanisms for supporting verifiable claims. arXiv:2004.07213.

Bostrom, N. (2017). Superintelligence: Paths, dangers, strategies. Oxford University Press.

Braverman, H. (1987). Labor and Monopoly Capital: The Degradation of Work in the Twentieth Century. Monthly Review Press.

Brynjolfsson, E., & McAfee, A. (2014). The second machine age: Work, progress, and prosperity in a time of brilliant technologies. WW Norton & Company.

Brynjolfsson, E., & Mitchell, T. (2017). What can machine learning do? Workforce implications. Science, 358(6370), 1530-1534.

Brynjolfsson, E., Mitchell, T., & Rock, D. (2018). What Can Machines Learn, and What Does It Mean for Occupations and the Economy? AEA Papers and Proceedings, 108, 43–47.

Chen, C., Li, Y., & Wang, S. (2016). A deep learning model for fraud detection in credit card transactions. IEEE Transactions on Neural Networks and Learning Systems, 27(8), 1872–1881.

Chen, H., Li, Y., Li, W., & Liu, T. (2016). Credit card fraud detection using deep learning based on convolutional neural networks. Journal of Intelligent & Fuzzy Systems, 31(1), 105-113.

Chollet, F. (2018). Deep Learning with Python. Manning Publications.

Crawford, K., & Calo, R. (2016). There is a blind spot in AI research. Nature, 538(7625), 311–313. https://doi.org/10.1038/538311a

Crosby, M., et al. (2017). Deep learning for financial time series prediction: Models and applications. Journal of Finance and Data Science, 3(2), 85–98.

Jiang, Z., Xu, D., & Liang, J. (2017). A deep reinforcement learning framework for the financial portfolio management problem. arXiv:1706.10059. https://doi.org/10.48550/arXiv.1706.10059

Davies, A. (2017). Autonomous vehicles and the future of urban tourism. Journal of Tourism Futures, 3(2), 133-137.

Demange, M., et al. (2019). Robotic mediation for the well-being of hospitalized elders with cognitive disorders. International Journal of Medical Informatics, 131, 103956. https://doi.org/10.1016/j.ijmedinf.2019.103956.

Chui, M., Manyika, J., & Miremadi, M. (2018). Notes from the AI Frontier: Insights from Hundreds of Use Cases. McKinsey Global Institute.

De Stefano, V., & Wouters, M. (2020). AI and digital tools in workplace management and evaluation: An assessment of the EU's legal framework. European Parliamentary Research Service, STOA.

Domingos, P. (2018). The master algorithm: How the quest for the ultimate learning machine will remake our world. Basic Books.

Eubanks, V. (2018). Automating Inequality: How High-Tech Tools Profile, Police, and Punish the Poor. New York: St. Martin's Press.

Doshi-Velez, F., & Kim, B. (2017). Towards a rigorous science of interpretable machine learning. arXiv preprint arXiv:1702.08608.

Esteva, A., et al. (2017). Dermatologist-level classification of skin cancer with deep neural networks. Nature, 542(7639), 115–118. https://doi.org/10.1038/nature21056

Eurogip. (2017). Collaborative robots: Issues and recommendations for prevention. https://www.eurogip.fr/publications/les-robots-collaboratifs-enjeux-et-recommandations-en-matiere-de-prevention/

Floridi, L., et al. (2018). AI4People—an ethical framework for a good AI society: Opportunities, risks, principles, and recommendations. Minds and Machines, 28(4), 689-707.

Eurofound. (2018). Automation, Digitisation and Platforms: Implications for Work and Employment. Luxembourg: Publications Office of the European Union.

Frey, C. B., & Osborne, M. A. (2017). The future of employment: How susceptible are jobs to computerisation? Technological Forecasting and Social Change, 114, 254-280.

International Labour Organization. (2023). World Employment and Social Outlook 2023. Geneva: ILO.

OECD. (2017). Tackling Wasteful Spending on Health. Paris: OECD Publishing.

OECD. (2024). OECD Employment Outlook 2024. Paris: OECD Publishing.

UNESCO. (2021). Recommendation on the Ethics of Artificial Intelligence. Paris: UNESCO.

World Economic Forum. (2020). The Future of Jobs Report 2020. Geneva: World Economic Forum.

Gautié, J., Jaehrling, K., & Pérez, Y. (2020). Technological change, new division of labour and job quality: Insights from French and German logistics warehouses. Transfer, 26(4), 417-433.

Golinelli, R., Rovelli, R., & Russo, A. (2020). The Impact of Artificial Intelligence on Employment in Europe. Social Indicators Research, 151(2), 435-456.

Goodfellow, I., Bengio, Y., & Courville, A. (2016). Deep Learning. MIT Press.

Gruson, D. (2019). Impact of Artificial Intelligence on Employment and Professions in the Health Sector. OECD Health Working Papers, No. 116. https://doi.org/10.1787/5e8481b1-en

Holm, J. R., & Lorenz, E. (2022). Task automation assessments and employment: A critical review. Research Policy, 51(1), 104394.

International Transport Forum (ITF). (2019). Managing the Transition to Driverless Urban Transport.

Jia, Y. (2019). The cost of deep learning: Financial and environmental impact. Journal of Computing Resources, 14(2), 45–61.

Katz, Y. (2020). Artificial Whiteness: Politics and Ideology in Artificial Intelligence. New York: Columbia University Press.

Jobin, A., Ienca, M., & Vayena, E. (2019). The global landscape of AI ethics guidelines. Nature Machine Intelligence, 1(9), 389–399. https://doi.org/10.1038/s42256-019-0088-2

Jordan, M. I., & Mitchell, T. M. (2015). Machine learning: Trends, perspectives, and prospects. Science, 349(6245), 255–260. https://doi.org/10.1126/science.aaa8415

Krafcik, J. (2021). Autonomous Vehicle Update. Waymo Blog. https://waymo.com/blog/autonomous-vehicle-update

Laurent, P. (2010). Mental fatigue. In E. Diener (Ed.), The Science of Well-Being (pp. 329–348). Springer.

LeCun, Y., Bengio, Y., & Hinton, G. (2015). Deep Learning. Nature, 521(7553), 436–444.

Lee, K. (2018). AI Superpowers: China, Silicon Valley, and the New World Order. Houghton Mifflin Harcourt.

McCarthy, J. (1956). Proposal for the Dartmouth Summer Research Project on Artificial Intelligence. Dartmouth College.

Moore, J. (2019). Human-robot collaboration in the workforce: Early findings from the field. In Companion of the 2019 ACM/IEEE International Conference on Human-Robot Interaction (pp. 85–86). IEEE.

Moore, P. (2019). Automating exploitation: Algorithmic decision-making and the gig economy. In E. Dowling & M. Taylor (Eds.), The Palgrave Handbook of Feminism and AI (pp. 201–217). Palgrave Macmillan.

Kolb, D. A. (1984). Experiential Learning: Experience as the Source of Learning and Development. Englewood Cliffs, NJ: Prentice-Hall.

Lipton, Z. C. (2018). The mythos of model interpretability. Communications of the ACM, 61(10), 36–43.

Marcus, G. (2020). The next decade in AI: Four steps towards robust artificial intelligence. arXiv:2002.06177.

Mazzucato, M. (2018). Mission-oriented research and innovation in the European Union: A problem-solving approach to fuel innovation-led growth. Luxembourg: European Commission.

Mittelstadt, B. D., Allo, P., Taddeo, M., Wachter, S., & Floridi, L. (2016). The ethics of algorithms: Mapping the debate. Big Data & Society, 3(2), 1–21.

Mokyr, J. (1990). The Lever of Riches: Technological Creativity and Economic Progress. New York: Oxford University Press.

Muro, M., Maxime, R., & Whiton, J. (2019). Automation and artificial intelligence: How machines are affecting people and places. Brookings Institution.

Obermeyer, Z., Powers, B., Vogeli, C., & Mullainathan, S. (2019). Dissecting racial bias in an algorithm used to manage the health of populations. Science, 366(6464), 447–453.

Patterson, D., et al. (2021). Carbon emissions and large neural network training. arXiv preprint arXiv:2104.10350.

Rajpurkar, P., et al. (2017). CheXNet: Radiologist-level pneumonia detection on chest X-rays with deep learning. arXiv preprint arXiv:1711.05225.

Rudin, C. (2019). Stop explaining black box machine learning models for high stakes decisions and use interpretable models instead. Nature Machine Intelligence, 1(5), 206–215. https://doi.org/10.1038/s42256-019-0048-x

Russell, S. J., & Norvig, P. (2010). Artificial Intelligence: A Modern Approach. Pearson Education.

Selbst, A. D., Boyd, D., Friedler, S. A., Venkatasubramanian, S., & Vertesi, J. (2019). Fairness and abstraction in sociotechnical systems. In Proceedings of the Conference on Fairness, Accountability, and Transparency (pp. 59–68). ACM.

Singhal, K., et al. (2023). Towards expert-level medical question answering with Med-PaLM. Nature, 620(7974), 526–535. https://doi.org/10.1038/s41586-023-06004-3

Startari, A. V. (2025a). AI Syntactic Power and Legitimacy: How AI Structures Shape Power. Working Papers No. 12. Montevideo: LeFortune. https://doi.org/10.5281/zenodo.17154108

Startari, A. V. (2025b). Executable Power: Syntax as Infrastructure in Predictive Societies. Zenodo. https://doi.org/10.5281/zenodo.15754714

Startari, A. V. (2025c). Colonization of Time: How Predictive Models Replace the Future as a Social Structure. SSRN Electronic Journal. https://doi.org/10.2139/ssrn.5284973

Startari, A. V. (2025d). Compiled Norms: Towards a Formal Typology of Executable Legal Speech. SSRN Electronic Journal. https://doi.org/10.2139/ssrn.5353059

Startari, A. V. (2025e). Grammar Without Judgment: Eliminability of Ethical Trace in Syntactic Execution. SSRN Electronic Journal. https://doi.org/10.2139/ssrn.5334549

Startari, A. V. (2025f). Template Power: How Instruction Templates Redistribute Decision Rights. Zenodo. https://doi.org/10.5281/zenodo.17879314 (also archived at https://doi.org/10.6084/m9.figshare.30849092; SSRN identifier pending)

Startari, A. V. (2025g). Foundation-Model Governance Pathways: From Preference Models to Operative Rules. Zenodo. https://doi.org/10.5281/zenodo.17533075 (also archived at https://doi.org/10.6084/m9.figshare.30589940; SSRN identifier pending)

Startari, A. V. (2026a). Plagiarism Ex Machina: Structural Appropriation in Large Language Models. Zenodo. https://doi.org/10.5281/zenodo.20070859 (also archived at https://doi.org/10.6084/m9.figshare.32204832; SSRN identifier pending)

Startari, A. V. (2026b). Algorithmic Empire: Generative AI and the Grammar of Global Subordination. Zenodo. https://doi.org/10.5281/zenodo.22096813 (also archived at https://doi.org/10.6084/m9.figshare.33329241; SSRN identifier pending)

Startari, A. V. (2026c). The Grammar of Asymmetric Visibility: AI, Zionism, and the Reallocation of Political Agency. Zenodo. https://doi.org/10.5281/zenodo.20271438 (SSRN identifier pending)

Steijn, W. M. P., Luiijf, E. A. M., & van der Beek, J. J. (2016). Robot assistants in elderly care: A mixed-method study on activities and perceptions. In European Conference on Cognitive Ergonomics (pp. 213–220). ACM.

VanLehn, K., et al. (2005). The architecture of intelligent tutoring systems. International Journal of Artificial Intelligence in Education, 15(3), 163–197.

Recht, B., Roelofs, R., Schmidt, L., & Shankar, V. (2019). Do ImageNet classifiers generalize to ImageNet? In Proceedings of the 36th International Conference on Machine Learning (pp. 5389–5400). PMLR.

Senge, P. M. (1990). The Fifth Discipline: The Art and Practice of the Learning Organization. New York: Doubleday.

Susskind, D. (2020). A World Without Work: Technology, Automation and How We Should Respond. London: Allen Lane.

Vaswani, A., Shazeer, N., Parmar, N., Uszkoreit, J., Jones, L., Gomez, A. N., Kaiser, Ł., & Polosukhin, I. (2017). Attention is all you need. In Advances in Neural Information Processing Systems 30 (pp. 5998–6008).

Veale, M., & Edwards, L. (2018). Clarity, surprises, and further questions in the Article 29 Working Party draft guidance on automated decision-making and profiling. Computer Law & Security Review, 34(2), 398–404.

Whittaker, M., Crawford, K., Dobbe, R., Fried, G., Kaziunas, E., Mathur, V., et al. (2018). AI Now Report 2018. New York: AI Now Institute.

Whittlestone, J., Nyrup, R., Alexandrova, A., Dihal, K., & Cave, S. (2019). Ethical and Societal Implications of Algorithms, Data, and Artificial Intelligence: A Roadmap for Research. London: Nuffield Foundation.

Yamamoto, K. (2019). Artificial intelligence and work: Evidence from Japan. RIETI Discussion Paper Series, 19-E-062.

Zawacki-Richter, O., et al. (2019). Systematic review of research on artificial intelligence applications in higher education. International Journal of Educational Technology in Higher Education, 16(1), 1–27.

Zhang, Y., Li, S., & Wang, J. (2021). Reinforcement learning in portfolio management: A survey. Journal of Economic Behavior & Organization, 190, 125–143.

INDEX

Did you love *AI, Tell Me Your Protocol*? Then you should read *Grammars of Power*[1] by Agustin V. Startari!

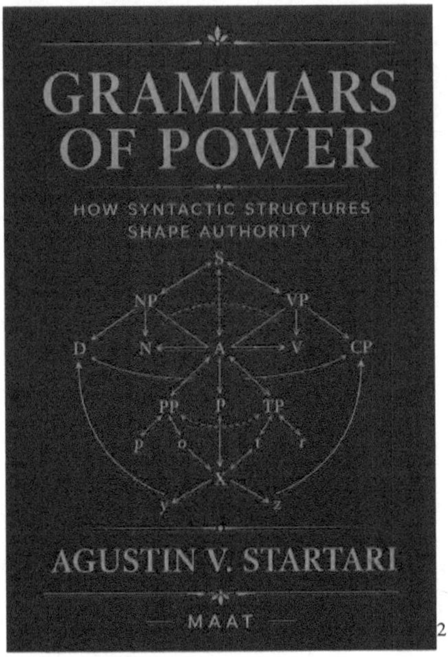

[2]

In a world where power is exercised through both weapons and words, *Grammars of Power: How Syntactic Structures Shape Authority* offers an unprecedented investigation into the relationship between the form of language and the exercise of domination. Spanning ecclesiastical, political, legal, and totalitarian discourse, this work demonstrates how grammatical choices—such as the use of passives, impersonal constructions, subordinate clauses, or deontic statements—are never neutral: they shape the perception of reality, obscure agents of power, and reinforce symbolic hierarchies.

From papal bulls to court rulings, from imperial proclamations to Nazi and Stalinist rhetoric, the book reveals that syntax is a political

1. https://books2read.com/u/mveNnl

2. https://books2read.com/u/mveNnl

technology as sophisticated as any system of physical control. Supported by tools from discourse analysis, formal logic, computational linguistics, and historical corpora, *Grammars of Power* offers a new critical perspective on the invisible mechanisms that regulate thought through language.

Combining theoretical clarity with academic rigor, this work not only examines the past, but also provides tools for interpreting the language of contemporary power—from algorithms to state discourse—at a time when words have once again become a battleground.

Work Papers is a publication series that brings together independent research on power, ideology, legitimacy, and history from a transversal and interdisciplinary perspective. Each volume stands as an autonomous work, while contributing to a common thread: the critical analysis of how power is structured, exercised, and sustained over time.

From Ancient Egypt to the totalitarian regimes of the twentieth century, from medieval theology to contemporary algorithms, this series explores the historical, linguistic, technological, and symbolic mechanisms that shape our societies. Power is understood here as a deep structure that traverses institutions, languages, myths, technologies, and bodies.

Each volume is numbered according to its place in this evolving series. *Working Papers* thus offers an intellectual architecture through which the reader can explore various forms of domination and resistance—from the most visible to the most invisible.

Read more at https://www.agustinvstartari.com/.

Also by Agustin V. Startari

Budismo Practico

Una vida de abundancia. La mente exitosa

Una mente abundante

Papeles de Trabajo

Creacion de un Imperio

La Alta Edad Media

Los Templarios: Marco introductorio

Gregorio X

Los apóstoles de la fe: en la pluma de Fray Bartolomé de las Casas

Maquinaria de Propaganda

Ucrania y Rusia: Un conflicto en progreso

Adios capitalismo

IA, dime tu protocolo

Gramáticas del Poder

IA Poder Sintactico y Legitimidad

Christus Solus

Herejías Esenciales: La lucha del cristianismo temprano

Fl Futuro como Origen

Practical Buddhism

The Path to happiness

A Wealthy Life: The Successful Mind

The Abundant Mind:

Work Papers

Creation of an Empire

THE EARLY MIDDLE AGES

The Templars: An Introductory Framework

Gregory X

THE APOSTLES OF FAITH IN THE WRITINGS OF FRIAR BARTOLOMÉ DE LAS CASAS

Propaganda Machinery

Ukraine and Russia: An Ongoing Conflict

AI, Tell Me Your Protocol

Ciao Capitalism: Reclaiming humanity beyond the Market

Grammars of Power

Christus Solus

Essential Heresies

Standalone

The year of the dead Count

Watch for more at https://www.agustinvstartari.com/.

About the Author

Agustin V. Startari is a researcher, linguist, and author specializing in the intersection of **language, artificial intelligence, power, legitimacy, and historical sciences**.

His work examines how linguistic, discursive, and technological structures organize perceptions of authority, distribute responsibility, and shape the ways institutions, artificial intelligence systems, and structures of power represent political, historical, and social events.

His research brings together **linguistics, discourse analysis, artificial intelligence, historiography, theories of power, and studies of legitimacy**, with particular attention to the relationship between linguistic form, authority, and political responsibility.

He is the author of the research series *Grammars of Asymmetric Visibility: AI, Imperial Power, and the Syntax of Responsibility*, focused on the relationships between artificial intelligence, language, power, and the attribution of responsibility.

He is also the author of *Work Papers*, a series devoted to historical research, historiography, and the analysis of problems related to the historical sciences.

Additional works include *Propaganda Machinery* and *Christus Solus*, which further explore the intersections of discourse, ideology, institutional power, and historical interpretation.

His work combines linguistic research, historical analysis, and the systematic study of the ways language, institutions, and technological systems participate in the construction and legitimization of power.

Read more at https://www.agustinvstartari.com/.

LEFORTUNE

PUBLISHING HOUSE

About the Publisher

LEFORTUNE Publishing is a distinguished international publishing house dedicated to the publication and global distribution of high-quality fiction, historical works, literary essays, cultural studies, and nonfiction in English, Spanish, and German. With a strong commitment to editorial excellence, intellectual depth, and cultural exchange, LEFORTUNE Publishing develops carefully curated titles for readers and institutions worldwide.

Read more at https://lefortunepublishing.com/.

www.ingramcontent.com/pod-product-compliance
Lightning Source LLC
LaVergne TN
LVHW100146061126
851857LV00010B/270
* 9 7 9 8 2 3 5 3 5 2 9 0 2 *